___ ᴜᴋ ᴏғ WALES
AND ITS CHURCHES

Revd John Parker's Tour of Wales and its Churches
(1798-1860)

Edgar W. Parry

TO MY WIFE
FOR MAKING THE WRITING
OF THIS BOOK POSSIBLE

ISBN: 0-86381-481-6

Cover design: Alan Jones

First published in 1998 by Gwasg Carreg Gwalch,
12 Iard yr Orsaf, Llanrwst, Wales LL26 0EH
☎ (01492) 642031
Printed and published in Wales.

Front Cover: Page from 'Snowdonia' by Lady Mary Leighton N.L.W.
Back Cover: Snowdon from Nantlle Lakes by John Parker   N.L.W.

Wales from H. Skrine's Tour of Wales 1798.

Contents

Acknowledgements

I am grateful for the assistance which I have received in the preparation of this book from many quarters and I would particularly like to mention the staff of the National Library of Wales, Aberystwyth at both the Manuscripts and Records Department and the Department of Pictures and Maps for the invaluable and ready assistance which they gave me at all times; the Revd Michael J. Walker B.A., Rector of Llanmerewig for giving me so much of his time and much useful information when showing me around the church at Llanmerewig; the Revd R.C. Ball for allowing me access to the church at Llanyblodwel; the Manager and staff of Sweeney Hall, near Oswestry; the Librarian, Oswestry Area Library and the Assistant Archivist, Lambeth Palace Library, London, and to Mrs Lavinia Bonnor-Maurice of Alberbury for copies of some of John Parker's drawings.

My special thanks are due to Sir Michael Leighton Bt. of Loton Park Shropshire for allowing me access to family papers in his possession and for his unstinting assistance with all my enquiries and also to Lady Leighton for her kindness and hospitality.

And finally my thanks are due to Gwasg Carreg Gwalch for publishing this work and for their helpful suggestions at all times.

Preface

'The stranger appears on the shadow'd hill,
And the foreign voice hath sounded there.'
'Snowdonia' by John Parker.

The period from 1750 to 1850 has quite rightly been referred to as the golden age of the English traveller in Wales. In some respects it is fortunate that so many of them published accounts of their journeys so that we today can have some understanding of the countryside as it was all those years ago, and at the same time experience some of the problems which faced those early travellers.

Writers like Thomas Pennant, William Bingley, Sir Richard Colt Hoare, Richard Fenton and Benjamin Heath Malkin need no introduction as their works are well known, but there are others who have made a considerable contribution to the literature of the travellers but are relatively unknown, and who deserve to be better known. The Reverend John Parker (1798-1860) certainly belongs to this category.

Parker wrote only one volume about his travels through Wales and that was entitled 'The Passengers' which he published in 1831. It is quite clear from reading his book, and his Journals at the National Library of Wales, Aberystwyth, that he was no ordinary traveller because of his various interests and the affection and understanding which he had of the country and its people.

His frequent visits to Snowdonia gave him a greater perception of the area than any other writer of his time. He was a prolific amateur artist and Snowdonia offered him unlimited scope for his artistic talent and his landscapes of the area depict its changing moods. Hundreds of his drawings and landscapes have also been deposited at the National Library of Wales.

He has enabled us to be cognizant of the neglected condition of the churches of Wales at the time, and he was travelling through the country before many of them were renovated in a manner which did untold damage to the fabric of many of the historical churches. He had visited every church in Wales which contained any vestige of Gothic ornament and made detailed observations upon them together with meticulous drawings of their screens, fonts, etc. But for these we would be unaware of the treasures which these early churches contained. He was the only person who toured Wales at that time on such an exhaustive undertaking.

He was also an amateur architect who had a passion for any form of Gothic architecture as was demonstrated by the work which he carried out on his churches at Llanmerewig in Montgomeryshire and Llanyblodwel in Shropshire. His architectural achievement did not please every one and some of the work which he carried out has since been destroyed. Nevertheless, his contribution was considerable and certainly merits consideration.

The purpose of this book is to examine his numerous tours through Wales and to record his observations on some of the many churches which he visited and to visualize them through his drawings and to appreciate that what was regarded as progress at the time of their renovation, did in effect, create untold harm.

I have considered it necessary to make a number of comparisons with other travellers, and this is done to highlight his approach to his tours and his understanding of Wales and at the same time to enable the reader to make a more balanced assessment of his contribution.

His personal accomplishments made him the perfect traveller at a time when so many travellers of indifferent abilities were touring Wales and publishing innumerable books about their experiences and which have now been long forgotten.

His journals make very interesting reading and contained within them are his own personal philosophies, expressed at times, with emotion and eloquence. The peace and quiet which he experienced amongst the mountains of Snowdonia were an inspiration to him. The solitude gave him the opportunity to examine his convictions dispassionately. Many of his Journals end with an acknowledgement that his knowledge and understanding of the area had been supplemented by his visits. In return, he presented us with a wonderful impression of Wales quite unlike any other traveller.

I have used the term 'traveller' in this book rather than 'tourist' since the latter has assumed a rather different connotation during the twentieth century.

To avoid confusion, the names of the Welsh counties found throughout this book are those which were in existence prior to the reorganisation of Local Government in 1974 so as to conform with the descriptions given by Parker.

I would like to think that this book will go some way to establish John Parker within the ranks of the very few remarkable travellers who came to Wales, and the bicentenary of his birth must surely be the most appropriate time to recognize his many achievements, for in him we have the traveller, writer, artist, architect and botanist embodied in one person.

Edgar W. Parry,
Caernarfon, 1998.

Chapter 1

The Parkers of Sweeney Hall

John Parker was the second son of Thomas Netherton Parker of Sweeney Hall near Oswestry. His mother was Sarah Browne, who as heiress of her uncle Edward Browne had inherited Sweeney Hall. His father died in 1848, and on the death of his mother he inherited the Sweeney Hall Estate.

The original Sweeney Hall was erected in 1640 when a Thomas Baker erected a 'new fair house in Sweeney, a handsome pile of buildings'. Thomas Baker died without issue in 1675 and the estate passed to a relative by the name of Thomas Browne. It was his grand-daughter who finally inherited the estate and married Thomas Netherton Parker in 1796. The original house was demolished in 1805 and the existing Hall was erected on the same site, and is of the late Georgian style. It is still completely in its original form. Only the pillars of the entrance gates and supporting walls remain of the original mansion.

The Parker family was an extremely gifted family. Thomas Netherton Parker was a noted antiquarian, architect and horticulturist and was highly respected in the border counties. He was an authority on cavalry and infantry subjects and on household economics and he wrote copiously on such subjects.

John Parker who had inherited his father's many talents, was educated at Eton and Oriel College Oxford where he graduated B.A. on 9th June, 1820 and M.A. on 9th June, 1825, and took Holy Orders.

It has been said that his health had never been very strong but his numerous tours of Wales would tend to dispel that idea. In his 'Shell Guide to Shropshire', Sir John Betjeman referred to him as a *'nineteenth century genius, man of letters and a cripple'*. But the very notion of him being a cripple must be entirely discounted. The state of his health, however, did mean that he had to leave Eton before finishing his education there.

On leaving Oxford he was ordained Curate of Moreton Chapel in Shropshire and in 1827 he was instituted by Dr Luxmoore, Bishop of St Asaph, to the rectory of Llanmerewig in Montgomeryshire. There was no Rectory at Llanmerewig and he resided in the farmhouse called Pennarth. It has been suggested that during the whole of his stay at Llanmerewig he had 'been buried in oblivion', but whilst it may have been true that it was a period tinged with sadness and frustration because of his inability to persuade his Bishop to allow him a Curate, he laboured ceaselessly in improving and adding to his church and this would have been a source of great satisfaction to him.

He had long shown a consuming interest in architecture and it was at Llanmerewig that he was first able to put his ideas into action. Despite his numerous and varied interests, it is perhaps for his interest in architecture that he is best remembered because he has left us a remarkable legacy of architectural drawings of screens and other church artefacts, many of which have disappeared or have been altered over the years due to over zealous church restorers. He had made drawings of all the screens in the churches of Wales and of all the chief types of baptismal fonts, although it must be emphasized that his architectural interest was confined solely to Gothic architecture. To him, there was no other style of architecture worthy of note.

He was firmly of the opinion that the architectural style of the thirteenth century in England, modified according to the practical requirements of the age, was the best adapted, both in construction and convenience. He was born at a time when very little interest was shown in church architecture and the churches were left completely un-cared for, but he remained firm in his conviction and he lived to see it bear fruit. He wrote:

'For of late, the long neglected Gothic has begun to command respect which a few years ago it never was thought likely to obtain – and seems likely to be followed through all its most expressive styles to a degree that until very lately seemed hopeless.'

Gothic architecture as he saw it, was inexorably tied to the Protestant religion and he was conscious that the increasing population demanded a large and continual supply of new churches, and the question as to what the style of their architecture should be, assumed more importance than ever to him.

'What are we to build? Are we to take the Italian churches for our models with their tall chimney-looking towers? or the Greek temples without windows? Does not every tolerably well informed man feel conscious that the only style of building which has a truly Christian appearance is that which in modern language we call Gothic? This beautiful art which was never known or understood in Rome, nor indeed in any part of Greece or Italy; is the peculiar boast and invention of Germany, France and England. It arose beyond the boundaries of classical architecture, and was carried on with perfect knowledge of what had already been done by the Greek and Roman architect.'

In 1835, when a new church was being built at Oswestry, he offered his services to the project, and as with all his other activities he gave it all that he could, including financial assistance. The chancel and vaulted apse he entirely undertook to build, and rich pendants and wood-vaulting similar to those at St David's Cathedral were used to overcome the radical difficulties which he encountered in a square interior. When working on his project he wrote:

'In undertaking to arrange and complete at my own expense, the ornamental furniture for the altar, pulpit, reading desk, font, gallery and roof in the new Chapel at Oswestry, my object has been to promote the majesty of public worship according to the forms of the Church of England by combining them with purest forms of Gothic art. The general style of the Chapel itself is that of the thirteenth century. My work will be designed in a transition style of the thirteenth and fourteenth centuries. No four-centred arch will be admitted in any part, and a large proportion of the canopies and traceries will be of cast iron, painted in dead oak colour.'

From Llanmerewig he was presented to the Vicarage of Llanyblodwel, Shropshire, in 1844, and it is here on the banks of the river Tanat that he has left the greatest and most lasting examples of his works.

Another abiding interest which almost equalled his love of Gothic architecture, was his love of plants. It must surely be one of the reasons why he made so may visits to the mountains of Snowdonia, for where better could he find the rare alpine plants which excited him so much. His Journals of Snowdonia contain numerous references to such plants and their location that even today his footsteps could be re-traced. But how many of the rare plants which he described can still be found there?

During his lifetime, the Victorian plant hunters were in vogue and at some time or another, they all arrived in Snowdonia in their perpetual search for rare plants and ferns. He was very conscious of their activities and the irreparable damage which they caused. During one of his early tours in 1820 he was at:

'The north west corner of Wythva where almost all the rare plants grow together in great abundance. Upon descending a few steps the profusion of blossoming plants which almost everywhere ornaments these 'Flowery rocks' agreeably surprised us. The most conspicuous was the Snowdon Pink (Silene acaulis) now in full flower, close to it in general view the opposite leaved saxifrage which had flowered in April, and in all quantities of it which we passed, we observed only one solitary flower. The seeds of course were not ripe. The other kind of saxifrage of white blossoms grew in large tufts or solitary specimens upon the rocks. The delightful fragrant Roseroot growing very large was in flower and in great plenty. We felt pleasure that their fortified situation so happily protected them from the rapacity and avarice of the seedsmen and the florists. For we know that other of our rarest native plants not so well guarded by nature have long ceased to ornament their native haunts.'

So wrote John Parker, the early conservationist, who had seen the dangers posed by some botanists whose main interest was in collecting as many specimens as possible to add to their collection with complete disregard to the true study of botany and the protection of plants. They were in reality mere 'plant collectors' and once they had acquired a particular specimen their interest in it soon abated.

He was also a remarkably competent artist, working mainly in water colours, and his numerous visits to Snowdonia enabled him to paint the mountain scenery in its various and changing moods. It is difficult to name any other single artist who has painted more views of Snowdonia than Parker. Snowdonia was not the only area which attracted him. He had travelled to Ireland, and Killarney provided him with equally romantic scenery as did the highlands of Scotland. His travels on the continent provided him with yet more subjects and his treatment of the Swiss glaziers demonstrates his artistic skills.

His artistic skill was used to the full in his flower painting or 'flower landscapes' as he used to refer to them He had little regard for the plethora of botanical prints; he always advocated that plants should be painted in their natural habitat:

'For scientific purposes, indeed as a means of learning the form of any plant or identifying it, when gathered, a coloured outline upon a page of white paper is not only sufficient, but the very best way of assisting the botanical student. Yet a solitary specimen upon a white background, is precisely that thing which we never see in real nature. Why is it that white flowers are so conspicuous? Because they are always thrown out, as it were, upon a coloured background.'

His success with his flower landscapes is quite apparent from his water colours at the National Library of Wales, Aberystwyth.

He was not the only accomplished artist in the family. His sister, Mary, who married Sir Baldwin Leighton, 7th Baronet of Loton Park, Shropshire in 1832, was also an artist of considerable merits and in many ways she excelled her brother. Some of her works are also deposited at the National Library. It was she who executed the exquisitely painted copy of his Gothic poem 'Snowdonia'. On his death, however, it was laid aside and she intimated that it would remain forever 'an unfinished work'.

The cultured and genteel background of an English country house was the ideal setting to nurture her artistic talents and she became a remarkably gifted and prolific artist. When Benjamin Disraeli stayed at her home at Loton Park in 1841 he described her as *'the finest amateur artist I know'*. But an inspection of her work today will lead one to say that she was the equal of many of the professional artists of her day. Her delicate water colours and portraits are a delight to see and demonstrate her remarkable talents.

Like her brother John, she painted scenes of Wales, and North Wales in particular. Many of her descendants also inherited her talents but to a lesser degree. She was also an extremely competent portrait painter and her delicate brush work is nowhere demonstrated better than in her portraits of her family and of her children in particular.

The Parker family were close friends of Lady Eleanor Butler and the Hon. Sarah Ponsonby, the celebrated 'Ladies of Llangollen'. John Parker's Journals contain many references of visits to their home at Plas Newydd.

The Ladies disliked the idea of having their portrait painted and had always refused requests for sittings. However, when Lady Mary Leighton accompanied her mother to Plas Newydd on one occasion she was able to make a quick sketch of them surreptitiously. This she was able to do while her mother engaged the Ladies in conversation.

She was unable to complete her portrait however, until after the death of the Ladies when she returned to Plas Newydd to complete the background. This is the only authenticate portrait of the Ladies. In it they are shown seated at an octagonal table with various artefacts on the table and with their cat seated on a chair beside it.

The picture was engraved on stone by R.J. Lane A.R.A., and prints were sold to Lady Leighton's friends in aid of alterations at Cardeston Church and various charities. However, a pirated version appeared showing the Ladies out of doors in riding habits and this resulted in legal action being taken to stop their sale. The print was eventually published as a Post Card by 'Valentines'.

It was Thomas Netherton Parker who designed the Ladies' tomb in the churchyard of St Collen's church, Llangollen.

Sir Baldwin and Lady Leighton had four daughters, Frances (Fanny), Isabella, Charlotte and Margaret, and two sons, Baldwin and Stanley who both became Members of Parliament.

Their four daughters were affectionately known as 'The Four Seasons' from a poem which had been composed and illustrated for them by Lady Leighton. It appears in a large decorated leather bound volume and consists of a page for each month depicting a landscape scene and borders of appropriate seasonal flowers surrounding each page.

She also executed a delightful poem by John Parker entitled 'The Upland Parish' describing the parish and church of Llanmerewig in Montgomeryshire. This again is a folio sized volume with scenes of the countryside surrounding Llanmerewig. The church itself appears in five of the six plates.

Music was another of her accomplishments and she was a gifted harpist and had a good contralto voice. She also wrote and produced a number of short plays for her family to perform on various occasions. These also appear in illustrated form and exquisitely painted. One such play is entitled 'The Bower of Truth'.

As the Revd John Parker was unmarried, the Sweeney Hall Estate passed to his sister Lady Mary Leighton on his death in 1860. She herself died of scarlet fever at Loton Park in 1864 aged 65. Sweeney Hall remained in the family until 1969 when it was eventually sold, having been in the family for over 300 years.

It is now an hotel.

Chapter 2

The Literary Works of the Travellers and 'The Passengers'

The result of John Parker's many tours of Wales was the publication in 1831 on his book *The Passengers* in which he described the Vale of Llangollen as ' . . . a fragment of heaven accidentally dropped upon earth', and many would agree with that description. It was the varied and wonderful scenery more than anything which drew the travellers to Wales. The wild mountain scenery of Snowdonia proved an attractive proposition and resulted in more tours through North Wales than any other part of the country.

It was the scenery of Snowdonia which attracted the artists and this at the time when great emphasis was placed upon 'the picturesque'. One of the greatest exponent of this subject was undoubtedly the Revd William Gilpin.

In 1773, Gilpin made a tour of North Wales and surprisingly enough he did not find Snowdon very picturesque. Gilpin was the author of *Observations on Picturesque Beauty* and *Observations on the River Wye and Several Parts of South* Wales. He was also the first topographer who reduced to certain rules the various 'combination of parts, the harmonies and the picturesque passages' of a landscape, and by so doing rendering the whole subservient to a science. He was in effect trying to prove that landscape gardening in some instances, was superior to nature. It was by these rules that he criticized Snowdon when he wrote:

'With regard to Snowdon, I fear not much can be said, as it nowhere appears connected enough as one whole to form a grand object, so neither has it any one of those accompaniments with which to form a beautiful one. It is a black and dreary waste, without any pleasing combination of parts, or any rich furniture, either of wood or well constructed rocks.'

Gilpin did admit, however, that he had never climbed Snowdon.

Subsequent writers and artists have rendered to Snowdon the homage which Gilpin denied, and none more so than Parker, who has painted more scenes of Snowdon than probably any other artist.

The Romantic Movement had also reached its zenith in England at the same time as the golden age of the travellers into Wales and the remote and mountainous regions were characteristic of the imagery of that Movement. 'Romantic' was also one of the most used adjectives of the English travellers and was used to distraction in their works. They often exaggerated their descriptions – all the mountains were 'extraordinary high' and the rocks and cliffs were 'too awful to comprehend'.

Between 1770 and 1839 about a hundred books were published about tours in Wales which at least demonstrate that the travellers felt some compulsion to write about their travels once they returned home. But what is the significance of these books today?

As can be expected, their literary value is very diverse. More often than not it is the personal prejudices of the writers which come to the fore. It can be said of quite a few of them that they came to Wales with certain preconceived ideas of what they expected to find, and then went ahead and wrote an account which conformed with those preconceived ideas.

Many weaknesses appear when the books are looked at critically. One weakness, if not the greatest, is the fact that the writers came for a period of two or three months at the most, and in that short period of time they firmly believed that they knew all that there was to know about Wales and its people, and consequently they felt that they could write with some authority on the subject. Whilst this may be quite clear to today's readers it was not so clear to the writers.

Edmund Burk was well aware of the problems that such a misconception might cause when he wrote 'The characters of nature are legible, but it is difficult for those who run to read them'.

The short period of their stay was not the only cause for their lack of knowledge. Another drawback was the fact that they did not understand the language, and English was not a language that was understood by many of the Welsh people. When all this is taken into consideration it is surprising indeed that so many of them felt confident enough to write about the character, culture and traditions of the Welsh as they did.

The comments of the author of *Walography, or the Briton Described* published in 1682 is typical of the contemptuous attitude of some travellers when he wrote:

'My remarks are spik and span new, and if they are ridiculous, they are not unlike the persons upon whom they are written. For the Welsh are a pretty odd sort of mortals, and I hope I have given you a pretty odd character of them.'

Despite its sarcastic comments, the book went into four editions, the last in 1749.

The conception of some travellers had changed very little by 1701 when *A Trip to North Wales* was published by one who called himself 'An Idle Lawyer'. This particular barrister had been given to understand that he could find a rich living in North Wales because the people were so predisposed to go to law.

His prejudices also come to the fore:

'The country looks like the fag end of creation, the very rubbish of Noah's flood, and will if anything, serve to confirm an Epicurean in his creed that the world was made by chance. Some suppose them (the Welsh) to be descended from the same common parents as us, but to hear one of them talk you would take them for some sort of pre-Adamites, nor can there be anything as troublesome as a Welshman when possessed with the spirit of Genealogy . . . Their houses generally consist of but one room, but that plentifully stocked with inhabitants, for besides the proprietors, their children and servants, you shall have two or three swine, and hard to say which are the greater brutes.'

When Louisa Costello published *The Falls and Mountains of North Wales* in 1839 she proclaimed that:

'part of the country called The Principality has been created by nature, in a holiday humour expressly for the recreation and delight of English tourists whose limited time did not allow them to seek for beauties abroad'.

Arthur Aikin on the other hand had quite different views. His tour in 1796 was specifically a geological excursion although his book deals more with topography than with the minerals he came to study. He writes little about the people and their customs and he acknowledges:

'That the requisite knowledge of a sufficient number of circumstances from which to deduce national character, is not to be acquired without a long residence, and much intercourse with the inhabitants. It is not to be gleaned in a hasty excursion through a country where its language, and the general shyness and suspicion which the natives discover towards the English or, to use their own words, the Saxons, oppose obstacles which only time and perseverance can overcome'.

19

Whilst the eighteenth century traveller was too ready to expose his prejudices, a few came later who wrote very condescendingly. In his *Sketches of Wales* (1826), the Revd G.J. Freeman wrote:

'I have never entered Wales in my life without a feeling of reverence for the soil on which I trod or rather I should say for that ancient race and those heroic deeds which has (sic) consecrated their soil in my imagination.'

By the late eighteenth century the travellers' literature was beginning to create some unease amongst the Welsh literati and in January 1776 Edward Williams (Iolo Morganwg) wrote to Owen Jones (Owain Myfyr) and informed him that he had acquired two new books but that he did not think very highly of them. One was *A Gentleman's Tour through Monmouthshire and Wales in the months of June and July, 1774* and the other *Letters from Snowdon* by Joseph Craddock (1770). He did not think that the books were worth purchasing but that they could provide some entertainment to Owain Myfyr if he had not already seen them. Iolo was of the opinion that he could have written a much better travel book than any which had been previously written if he could only spend a few weeks in North Wales to supplement the information which he already possessed. Despite numerous visits to North Wales Iolo's book never materlized.

In 'The Cambrian Register' for 1796 there appeared a critical analysis of some of the books on Welsh tours by a writer who called himself 'Cymro' (Welshman). In this article 'Cymro's' severest criticism was that the writers did not understand the language and neither had they spent sufficient time in Wales to acquaint themselves of the country and its people. According to 'Cymro' the only writer who had sufficient knowledge was Thomas Pennant.

The three travellers referred to specifically by this correspondent were Henry Skrine, Richard Warner and Arthur Aikin. Skrine was criticized because of his literary style and neither did he excel as a traveller because:

'his style abounds with metaphors and epithets, singularly and affectedly applied, and frequently extravagantly conceived and oddly expressed; he talks of intervals in a mountainous ridge in Monmouthshire forming a succession of valleys like the cells of a honeycomb; buildings at Llantrisant, clustered like a swarm of bees and hills floating with water and feathering woods'.

Warner of the other hand was criticized for making his tour on foot and his 'silly and ridiculous whim of converting pleasure into toil'. He was also accused of mis-spelling Welsh names although it must be added that Warner was not the only writer guilty of this.

Aikin is congratulated upon the accuracy of his spelling but is criticized for not mentioning anything about Welsh life and customs – although as I have previously stated, it was not his intention to write upon such matters because he lacked the necessary qualifications.

It is quite possible that today's readers would find 'Cymro's' tirade strange and his arguments frivolous, but in the context of the period it is important to be conscious of them. His comments were considered relevant at the time and they reflected the opinions of many of his contemporaries.

Very few of the early writers took much notice of copyright, and many of them borrowed long extracts from the works of others without acknowledgement. Many have also been criticized for using extracts from the works of Thomas Pennant although he in turn was also guilty on occasions. Care must therefore be taken when reading these early works because errors made by one writer could well have been perpetuated by another.

A cursory glance through the early literature will show that many of them do nothing other than repeat what had been written before, whilst others merely give a simple and tedious account of a journey from one place to the next with no detailed descriptions. Despite the fact that so many books have been written about tours in Wales, very few of them have any real merit.

In 1856, Julius Rodenberg came to North Wales and he stayed for some time at Wern, a farm at Abergwyngregin in Caernarfonshire. His book *Ein Herbst in Wales* translated by Dr William Linnard gives a delightful account of his stay. Rodenberg was no ordinary traveller and he came to Wales to study the country and its people from a German perspective, and he makes many illuminating and entertaining observations on Welsh customs. He also translated some of the Welsh folk songs into German.

Towards the end of his stay he described the wedding of Sarah, the daughter of Wern, in some detail and all in accordance with the customs of Welsh weddings, but Dr Linnard shows that Sarah did not marry during Rodenberg's stay. What Rodenberg did was to collate all the customs relating to Welsh marriages there were known to him and attribute them to Sarah's wedding. This does not, however, detract from this delightful book but merely serves as a caution when reading such books.

Parker's contribution to this literature was his book *The Passengers* which was published in 1831. In many respects this book is quite different from any other on Welsh tours. The book is in the form of a dialogue between three imaginary characters and to these characters he has given classical names of 'Clanvoy', 'Larndon' and 'Allansley', a popular practice at the time but short lived, and it is quite clear from the ensuing dialogue that Parker himself is 'Clanvoy' because he is the guide and the one who is able to answer all the questions asked by the other two characters.

On a fine summer morning at the end of July in the 1820's the three 'outside Passengers' left Oswestry by one of the early morning coaches for Capel Curig embarking on a tour through North Wales. 'Clanvoy' explains to his two companions 'that no man living has been more assiduous in exploring the wilds of Snowdonia. Long before and after Eton and Oxford, I travelled there. For several years together I always made one tour in that neighbourhood, if not more, and whenever I went there, it was by this road'. Parker had set the stage and declared 'Clanvoy' to be the leader of the expedition.

In establishing the style of his book, it becomes clear that Parker had a thorough knowledge of Snowdonia and his frequent visits had enabled him to write with some authority and compassion – a trait not commonly found amongst other travellers. It is not only the beauty of the landscape which enthrals him but he quickly displays his knowledge and interest in botany as he travels over the Berwyn mountains.

His interest in Gothic architecture comes to the fore as soon as he sees one of the ancient churches on his route. In general he described the churches as the 'chief barn of the neighbourhood', but even so, he is keen to point out that they could have some attraction. In places where he found no pretensions to Gothic art in the stonework of the building he would meet with wood carving so exquisite and original that if it were found in some English Cathedral the lover of Gothic would be in raptures of admiration. He discounted the idea that Gothic art was intimately connected with 'monkish errors and the corruptions of Roman Catholic idolatry'. He looked upon Gothic niches, shrines and all the ornamental appendages of saint-worship as wonders of art from which he could learn much as to the details of decoration in churches. That they had been used for idolatrous customs was regrettable, but he was only anxious to prove that Gothic art was not of necessity connected with popery.

As he approached Llangollen he could see the ruins of Valle Crucis Abbey in the distance with its grey walls and roof with their splashes of yellow lichen and one tall narrow Gothic window. The central tower and its arches had fallen many years before 'in those days when nobody knew or cared much about the styles of sacred architecture'. But to him the whole ruin contained elements of exquisite workmanship and design and the marigold window in the west end could not have been improved upon in any way.

At Corwen he could not resist the temptation to vent his feeling against Owain Glyndŵr 'that outrageous destroyer of Gothic' and in particular for the fact that he had gone out of his way to destroy the Abbey of Cwm Hir in Radnorshire which he considered to have been the grandest of all Welsh Abbeys and equalled any first-rate English Cathedral.

Owain Glyndŵr's parish church at Corwen did not fill him with enthusiasm but he felt that its white washed tower would be improved by the insertion of Gothic windows and some pinnacles at each corner.

The coach had stopped for some little time at Corwen and when it was time to proceed and the coachman had mounted his box in front of the Owain Glyndŵr Inn, the 'Passengers' resumed their seats and left the grey and white houses of the town behind them.

The journey continues and the 'Passengers' now talk of the landscape. Gothic architecture has been forgotten for a while. In the distance they saw a white painted parish church with its distinctive belfry and two or three gigantic old yew trees growing near it, and far beyond, with endless variation of light and shadow, mountain ranges came to view.

Arrival at the coaching Inn of Cernioge was always a significant occasion for Parker. Cernioge was an important staging post for all travellers, it was here that the horses were changed and it was here that he always experienced his heart beating faster because he could see the mountains of Snowdonia beckoning him; the pointed summits of Snowdon and Moel Siabod, Glyder Fawr and Glyder Fach, Carnedd Dafydd and Carnedd Llewelyn – they all had a very special attraction for him. He once referred to his visits as 'extending over a period of nearly half a century, during which time as a thoroughbred mountaineer I became familiar with all the wildest localities of Snowdonia'. He was always conscious of the beauty of the mountains, not for him 'the awful terror' nor the 'unspeakable heights' referred to so often by other travellers, and in all his tours he felt that the mountains held a special charm for him and their silence made it profane to talk.

At Betws-y-coed he noticed the pine trees with their stiff austerity utterly destroying all the character of 'romantic luxuriance that other trees give to a mountain landscape. If they were common in Wales the country would not be worth looking at. These lower mountains cannot overcome such blemishes. We deal here in fantastic beauty'. How very prophetic his comments appear today!

At half past two after a tiring journey of seven hours the 'Passengers' arrived at their destination – Capel Curig – and they were shown into a large parlour, a room 'hung around with maps and magnificent engravings from the pictures of Rubens'. They immediately sat down to a dinner of trout from the Ogwen lake with 'that peculiarly high flavour, which for want of a more expressive term I shall term *Alpine*'. Here they were entertained at dinner by Evan Jones, the harper, who played a selection of Welsh airs. Evan Jones was also a noted guide provided by the Inn for the benefit of travellers.

After dinner, tired though they were, they explored the lower slopes of Glyder Fach, about a quarter of a mile from the Inn and discussed their arrangements for ascending Snowdon the following day.

Glyder Fach was a source of inspiration to him when he was writing his Gothic poem 'Snowdonia' when he likened the massive rocks on the summit to the choir of Cologne Cathedral:

> Wondrous are the scenes around thee
> Thou beholder of the hills!
> Where the cloud hath slowly found thee
> Resting in their lonely cells!
> O! What art, or workman equals
> Their spires of lofty stone?
> Like the richly wrought Cathedrals,
> Like the Choir of Cologne!
> From the mountain height ascending,
> Each in arrowy sharpness ending –
> Though the lightning fiercely rend them
> Firm remains yon stately cone!

In adopting the narrative form for the book he is able to proceed from one subject to another with ease and a discussion on Gothic architecture can be readily interspersed with botanical observations or comments on the landscape. He must be the only traveller to have adopted this particular form of writing and it gives the reader an insight into his many interest and indeed, to become the 'fourth passenger' albeit a silent one, and at the same time share in the enjoyment of the others.

The journey to the summit of Snowdon on this occasion was in effect a botanical excursion where he visited various sites to look for rare alpine plants. This section demonstrates his knowledge as a botanist and his keen interest in the subject. At the time when the Victorian plant hunters were most active in Snowdonia he was already conscious of the danger that many rare plants would disappear for ever. When at Clogwyn y Garnedd he writes 'several of the plants mentioned as growing here a few years ago, either never did, or have been utterly destroyed. They have possibly been carried off by the numerous explorers of that rock, for, steep as it is, there is hardly any part of it which an active botanist would not reach, by taking time and care. It is full of clefts and ledges, just enough to hold by, or to rest the foot on, and botanical eyes are too much engaged in the details of each fissure to look at the height or depth of it'. It was his understanding of botany that made him an early conservationist.

The Passengers sets Parker apart from other writers on a number of points. His numerous excursions into Snowdonia gave him the necessary knowledge and authority to write such a book; he writes with sympathy and an understanding of the country and its people and he can understand why the people are different, and indeed, their right to be different. Although he did not speak Welsh never once did he ridicule the people for not speaking English – a criticism which can be levied against a large majority of the early travellers. He came to Wales with an open mind and a willingness to learn about the country and its people. He was also well prepared for his visits in that he was conversant with the history of the country and the problems which it had to face. Yet, his sympathy and understanding never stooped to condescension. With the publication of *The Passengers* he made a worthy contribution to the literature of the travellers. The greater part of the book had been published in the *Cambrian Quarterly Magazine* and the reception which it had received at the time encouraged him to publish it in book form. It is unfortunate that the book is now so scarce that a wider readership could not enjoy it. Although the book is shown as 'Volume One' a second volume did not materlize.

Apart from *The Passengers* Parker left a large number of Journals describing his various tours. These are now in the National Library of Wales, Aberystwyth, and form the basis of the tours which I have described in this book.

When discussing the literature of the travellers it is important that unpublished manuscripts be also studied with equal care. Many of these disclose their authors' characteristics which may not be so apparent in their published works. The manuscripts were never intended for publication but rather for private circulation amongst families and friends. Consequently they will reveal more than what an author would intend for publication. Many of them are disparaging and underline their authors' prejudices and dislikes more than anything else. The passage of time, however, has an ameliorative effect and they now make very amusing reading.

Chapter 3

St Llwchaiarn Church, Llanmerewig

In 1827, at the age of 29, John Parker became Rector of the Parish of Llanmerewig near Newtown, Montgomeryshire, having spent a short period as Curate of Moreton Chapel, near Oswestry. Here he remained until he was presented to the vicarage of Llanyblodwel, Shropshire, in 1844.

The church at Llanmerewig is dedicated to St Llwchaiarn to whom two churches in Cardiganshire are dedicated as well as the neighbouring church of Llanllwchaiarn near Newtown. It is beautifully situated on the ridge of a hill overlooking the Severn Valley and within a circular cemetery.

It has been suggested that these circular cemeteries have been influenced by the early Celtic churches. It is quite likely that the Druids, after their conversion to Christianity acted as priests of the new faith, and in such cases it was not unnatural that they would continue to officiate in their ancient Druidical Circles. Circular churchyards dating back to the sixth centuries are not uncommon in Wales. Other examples within Montgomeryshire are to be found at Llanerfyl and Llangadfan and at Diserth in Radnorshire. Another widely held view was that they were made circular so that there would be no corner for the Devil to hide in!

This small mediaeval church with a bell-turret at the west end of the roof, a small south porch and the whole white washed as was so often the case, was in a poor and unsafe condition when Parker arrived there. He soon set out with gusto to undertake the necessary repairs largely to his own designs and at his own cost.

He had an interest in Gothic architecture, and at Llanmerewig he had the first real opportunity to put his ideas into action. Looking around the church today is an interesting experience because by so doing it is possible to follow the progress of his repairs and additions by his practice of dating everything that he did. The tower for example, has two dates: the lower section is dated 1838 and the top section is dated 1839, whilst the new south porch is dated 1840 and a window surround in the south wall is dated 1843.

In 1838 when he was embarking upon further alterations, the population of the parish at the 1831 census was 201; the church would accommodate 140 people and the congregation in general averaged 90. The congregation, however, was much increased by the attendance of persons from the outskirts of neighbouring parishes, who lived much nearer to Llanmerewig than to their own parish church. His proposed new belfry would have enabled him to provide about fourteen additional places. He was of the opinion that an additional building equal in size to the original would eventually be necessary. The west wall of the church had been built in so loose a manner that it warranted immediate repair and his intended belfry would act as a buttress to it.

Although a church of small proportions, being only 50 feet long by 18 feet wide and 17 feet high, some of his additions were quite substantial, for example, the large two-decker pulpit-cum-reading desk which he designed would have been out of proportion for such a small building. It did however, conform to his perception of the pulpit being a place of exhortation rather than prayer. It admitted varieties in the performance of the duties peculiar to it, according to the character and talents of the preacher and, therefore, it claimed a more elevated situation. His view was that:

'In the sermon, the congregation are not prepared for what follows, let the preacher therefore have every possible advantage of the situation, that his looks and gestures as well as his voice may render his meaning clear to those who are farthest from him. There is only one place in my church where the pulpit ought evidently to be, that is in a spot where most can see and hear the preacher and where he may receive a steady light.'

His pulpits both at Llanmerewig and at Llanyblodwel conformed to those ideal.

On the 2nd May, 1838, he wrote for financial assistance from the Incorporated Church Building Society, and he stated:

'In 1833 I began to build a singers' gallery, and since then I have been constantly engaged in various improvements, external and internal, the expense of which has almost entirely fallen upon myself. A vestry has been built and I should also mention that whatever has been done within that period has been done with strict attention to ecclesiastical style. Two galleries are now built capable of accommodating about 20 persons each, and the chancel, which was becoming unsafe, has been secured by a massive diagonal buttress at each corner. These repairs were carried on with great care, and are designed in the plain but pure Gothic of the 13th century. We cannot however, take full advantage of these improvements without removing the wooden belfry which is on the west wall of the church, and building a new stone one beyond that wall. The rain beats in through the windows of our present belfry and injures the ceiling and wall of the new gallery below it.'

He ended his letter by stating that he was in the habit of superintending such work himself, and that every new example of early church Gothic then being erected enabled the Society to have their designs better executed in the future by improving public taste and the ability of the workmen. The assistance which the Society might give would 'never be so usefully bestowed as in those cases where the incumbent of the parish will see to its being applied efficiently'.

The plans and estimates for his new stone belfry were prepared by a Mr Newman, an architect from Newtown, and the cost was £100. Parker had received subscriptions from the parishioners, non-resident landlords and neighbours amounting to £40, and he was requesting a grant of £60 to complete the project. In support of his application he wrote:

'In the hope that it may strengthen my appeal, I can assure the Society that I am contributing largely to the building of other churches in which I have no professional interest, and that more than my clerical income is devoted to this purpose, at Llanmerewig and elsewhere.'

In February 1840 he again wrote to the Incorporated Church Building Society confirming that the work on the belfry had been completed. The work had taken longer than anticipated to complete 'because the length of time required for the production of any real Gothic work and the difficulties with regard to the carriage of materials'. He then proceeds to give an interesting account of the decorations within the church:

'My church abounds with inscriptions, and of the black letter, and it is an object with me to exclude the Roman alphabet. There is more ornament than is perhaps usual these days in the ceilings, galleries, and in some external parts of my church. This however, has resulted not from any large means of any kind, but merely from the fact that I am in the habit of designing and setting such work and execute it partly myself. The new front of the porch is in the transition style from the Anglo-Norman to the Early Gothic. The belfry is 10 or 12 feet higher than was at first intended, and is in the style of the thirteenth century.

In building the vestry, and adding the new front porch, I gave the plans and superintended the work myself, but for the chancel, buttresses and the belfry, I engaged the professional services of Mr Newman, the architect residing in the neighbourhood, without whose concurrence I should have hardly ventured on giving to my belfry the proportions of an Italian campanile.'

He was, however, always striving for perfection and re-evaluating his work to see if it could have been better designed and executed, and of the tower at Llanmerewig he wrote 'were I to build the tower over again, the upper part should certainly be finished off like the bell turret of my school, because the latter looks well from every point of view, Llanmerewig, on some sides only'.

From the above, it is quite clear that Parker belonged to a select group of Clergymen of his period who took an active and positive approach to the repair of the fabric of their churches and who were capable of undertaking and financing much of the work themselves.

He was also mindful of the comfort of his parishioners in that he installed a fireplace against the south wall with an elaborate Gothic chimney. He had taken great care in the design of the chimney and he once wrote that he had 'occasion to consult all the best known examples but met with none more exquisite than the one at Grosmont, Monmouthshire'. But even that proved to be not as rich as the one he had designed and would not have suited him so well. This chimney he considered 'the most elaborate ever made, there is something like it at Lichfield but lost among the pinnacles, and I think in my early youth I saw something like it at Bangor'.

His alterations and additions were not to everyone's taste and when further restorations were carried out in 1892 many of his original ideas were considered unsuitable and consequently removed. The Gothic chimney was taken down and the stones used to replace another chimney at the vestry and sections of it are still being used as flower containers on either side of the footpath leading to the church door.

He had concealed the original ceiling with a rounded plaster ceiling and when this was removed the fine 14th century roof which can be seen today was brought to light.

The two-tiered pulpit-cum-reading desk was dismantled and the galleries were removed with some of the carved wood work being used in the construction of a new screen. The inscriptions which 'abounded and of the black letter' as referred to by him in his letter above were also removed.

Whilst it may have been necessary in 1892 to effect some further alterations, it is unfortunate that all the inscriptions were removed as it is possible that modern eyes would be less offended by his idiosyncratic style. Nevertheless, his unique style and flair can still be seen and admired in his church at Llanyblodwel.

Successful though he may have been as Rector of Llanmerewig, it would appear from his writings that his stay there was tinged with sadness and his great effort in restoring the church had taken its toll upon him. He felt that he should have a Curate to shoulder some of the responsibility.

In September, 1832 he went to see the Bishop of St Asaph to seek his assistance, but to no avail. He wrote:

'After waiting a few minutes, I saw the Bishop and consulted with him to little purpose for almost an hour. I could not accomplish my object, and he threw objection in my way of all that I proposed without expressing the slightest intention (the question between us concerned the appointment of a Curate with a salary below £90, but in proportion to the small value of the living). I had luncheon at the Palace and wished his Lordship good morning. I have sacrificed much to the church already and if it had been in my power would sacrifice yet more.

I saw the monument to the late Bishop, who had he lived, might have done something for me, but his giving me my present living was a gift that I would rather not have accepted. Alas, how difficult it is to obtain even a moderate income in the Church of England; how lowering and vexatious are the embarrassment that surround us. I call my living a popish living, for it forbids me to marry, and if I had not other means it would almost command me to abstain from meat.'

In 1844, he was presented to the vicarage of Llanyblodwel, Shropshire, and embarked upon another period of great activity in the service of the church.

Chapter 4

The Upland Parish (Llanmerewig) by the Revd John Parker

A lovely land in mine to me
A lovely land is mine,
A land that I rejoice to see
Half earthly half divine.
A cloud is on the lonely moor,
A gleam is on the vale
It lights the hamlet of the poor
And ornaments the dale.

Tall are the trees that rise around
The hedgerows and the grove,
The Poplar on the marshy ground
The nobler Oak above.
And Oh! beyond yon green retreat
That lures the searching eye
How oft the mountains dimly meet
The vapour of the sky.

Yon stream flowing so bright along
There owns a lofty fount
And learns to chant its hasty song
Within that airy mount.
A dreamy light, a wild repose
A calmness undefined
These lead the heart from earthly woes,
And captivate the mind.

There are pleasant woodland meadows
Fill'd with budding flowers,
There are thickets deep in shadows
Wild and solemn bowers.
There are desert moorland hollows
Higher yet and higher,
Glens which the bright sunbeam hallows
Oft with living fire.

But first of all and last of all
My heart returns to thee,
Thou mansion of the Almighty Lord,
Who died upon the tree.
Thy low but ancient walls adorn,
Yet more the flow'ry green,
They consecrate each breezy lawn
They bless the lovely scene.

Though far from eastern realms away
And in the cloudy west,
Yon lonely church invites to pray
The least is as the best.
In every place where shall be found
The righteous and the true,
Their earthly haunt is Holy ground.
To them, to me, to you.

By kind permission of Sir Michael Leighton, Bt.

Chapter 5

The Church of St Michael the Archangel, Llanyblodwel

In 1844, John Parker became Vicar of Llanyblodwel in Shropshire. The church is dedicated to St Michael the Archangel, and although of Norman foundation only the south doorway remains of the original building. It is situated in the beautiful and peaceful Tanat Vale and it still retains the same tranquillity as it did in the days of Parker himself.

In an ante-room above the vestry there is a stone tablet inscribed 'This school-house was erected Ao.D 1719'. There cannot be many churches where the school master's house and school room were under the same roof as the church.

On his arrival he was faced with exactly the same problems as he had faced at Llanmerewig in that the church was in a deplorable condition, so much so, that the south wall was in urgent need of attention and was nearly falling down. He found that the repairs could only be effected by the demolition and complete rebuilding of the wall. After his experiences at Llanmerewig he was quite confident that he could undertake this project himself and it was a task which he undertook with great enthusiasm, and this time he did not employ the services of an architect. It is interesting to note that during his time at Llanyblodwel he did not once consult with the Church Building Society with regard to any of the alterations which he carried out there.

Additional accommodation was also required within the church and he proposed to incorporate the school room within the church and provide a new school and schoolmaster's house on another site. The cost of almost all the alterations and additions to the church and the building of the school and school master's house were met by Parker himself and amounted to about £10,000.

Here again, as at Llanmerewig, he has dated all the alterations which he carried out and the south wall and windows are dated 1847, the dormer windows 1850 and 1853 and the porches 1849 and 1851 and the tower was built in 1855.

With regard to the school-house, he wrote to his niece Frances on the 2nd March 1859:

'I am going on successfully with my school master's house, floors and doors are in hand, also chimneys, which are looking good, and two days ago, tempted by a new subject, I began to sketch in the open air. On Monday I hope to get most of the scaffolding down and then it will be seen what I mean by a Gothic house, a thing which I could not otherwise explain. The closing of this long job, will, I suppose leave me at more leisure that I have been for two years.'

He was particularly proud of the east window in the school house as 'it was a form very nearly approached in the Gothic era but never attained, I have long sought it', but here he attained it and considered it a successful conclusion to the project.

By 1859 his health was deteriorating rapidly and a cursory inspection of the church today will show the visitor that his contribution had been considerable. The result of all his hard work had taken its toll upon his health.

The two most notable things that will fascinate the visitor will be the internal decorations and the tower with its domical spire.

In September of 1836 he had made a tour of South Wales and had visited the Cathedral of St David's in Pembrokeshire. This was certainly the highlight of this particular tour and he was quite captivated with the Cathedral. According to his Journal he wandered up and down quite subdued by the grandeur of it and finding himself incapable of drawing any part of it. He described the ceiling with its twenty six highly wrought pendants suspended in two rows from one end of the nave to the other, and between them, the ceiling arranged in squares and panelled. This was a scheme which he decided to adopt in the woodwork for the vaulting of a small oriel in the chancel of the church at Llanmerewig.

It was also a scheme which he adopted for the decoration of the church at Llanyblodwel. Here we see him at his most extravagant best. Again he adapts the style which fascinated him so much at St David's and, in accordance with his custom, the date 1847 appears on one of the bosses. The roof is richly coloured and divided into panels and ornamented with pendant posts and carved bosses.

The reredos and altar table are all profusely decorated and coloured in accordance with Gothic principles which were so important to him in blue, red and gold. On the walls are numerous Scripture quotations in 'the black letter' which he admired so much. The decorations around the windows and on the arches between the two aisles are certainly of his own design as also is the altar table which he copied from a design which he saw on a tour of Italy and which he executed himself.

Here as at Llanmerewig he was to reassess the work which he had carried out. He considered that 'the ribs of the chancel ceiling are too large, they diminish the height, but the mouldings are the richest that can be made in wood'.

His decorations here, as at Llanmerewig, were not to everyone's taste and they were subsequently covered over when the interior was white washed at the turn of the century. However, everything was not lost because in the restoration scheme carried out in 1959-1960 the removal of the white wash revealed the glory of his original decorations in almost perfect condition.

Here also he had built a two-decker pulpit as at Llanmerewig but not quite so elaborate, and that has also been removed. The prayer desk portion of it was re-erected to form the pulpit which is now in use. The whereabouts of the remainder of the original pulpit is unknown.

The work which he carried out was not always without difficulties. On Christmas Eve, 1856, he described the completion of the wheel window which he placed in the gable of the west end of the church:

'This window is the first example of wire foliation combined with actual tracery. It is a circle of five feet in diameter internally but only four feet in tracery which is nine inches thick, and near the outside wall so as to leave two feet for the inner splay, the wall itself being one yard thick. A succession of dry temperate and almost warm days during the past fortnight has been of great use to our operations, indeed had the weather been otherwise than fair, we could not have carried on the work even if we had ventured on beginning it. I rejoice at having completed this difficult work at such a hazardous time of the year. For altho' Christmas day was fine in the morning, the weather changed in the afternoon and the day after was very tempestuous. The snowstorms of yesterday have now been succeeded by hard frost.

After the stonework of the tracery had been built and glazed, an alarming accident occurred which might have been a very serious one. The inner circle is composed of 16 stones each two feet long and less than a foot wide, but larger at one end than the other on account of the splay. Thirteen of these had been already set and were supported on props until the rest of the circular arch could be inserted. At this moment, part of the old wall above, which had been cut through in order to introduce the new window, fell down and carrying with it the props, and four of the 16 stones lost their hold and fell upon the inner

35

scaffold! They were prevented going down upon the pavement of the church by the props which lay across an opening in the scaffold. Happily none of the workmen were inside, and outside there was only John Vaughan who was not in any danger. The stones were damaged in some of their edges but none were cracked through, and after a little additional working they took their place as before.'

It would have been no mean task to cut through an old stone wall a yard thick!

On 15th December, whilst opening the west wall for the wheel window, his workmen found three fragments of Sweeney Mountain stone embedded in the rough masonry. They were portions of an ancient slab 8 inches in thickness and had once formed the tombstone of some chieftain or other.

A previous vicar, the Rev. William Worthington in 1736 described the chancel screen as extending across the nave and north aisle and containing arcading of eighteen bays, with similar tracery in each compartment. This screen was again considerably repaired and renovated by Parker. He considered the panels to be 'the most successful work in the church, and they cost me much labour'.

His most difficult, demanding and rewarding task must have been the erection of the tower and spire by the west wall which he undertook in 1855-1856.

He was anxious that the tower should make an impression on all who saw it and with this in mind he made widespread researches to find something which would comply with his ideas. Not for him, this time, the square shaped tower of Llanmerewig, nor the grand spire of Salisbury Cathedral which John Constable had once described as 'suddenly dart into the sky like a needle'. After careful deliberation he settled on a spire on the general outline of 'the German Fribourg, with the domical curvature, though difficult and rare form, is geometrically stronger than that of the straight-sided spire. In the alternate arrangement of the windows, the example of Sedegeberrow, a Gloucestershire church has been copied. The same distribution of windows occurs in the Keep Tower of the Early English Castle of Stokesay'. He felt confident that this would be the noblest and strongest of all for his church at Llanyblodwel.

It was a design, however, that was fraught with problems for him, and in his diary for 2nd January, 1856, he wrote:

'Yesterday and today I have been trying to strike the curve intended for the sides of my spire. It is very difficult. I have not yet succeeded. The radius of the circle according to my drawing (done to scale) should be 230 feet. The ground of the field is not quite level, we have tried pack thread: we have tried laths nailed together, but we cannot get the curve exactly, which in a perpendicular height of 45 feet is to be, half-way up, one foot from the inclined straight line, which is 46 feet. I do not see how it can be struck unless I get some copper bell-wire of that length.'

By perseverance, he had by 19th January 'on this day, in the midst of cold and wet, we at length succeeded in striking the curved outline of the spire'. The work then continues apace.

Just a week before this final obstacle had been surmounted he felt confident enough to celebrate by giving 'a second dinner to the waggoners and under-waggoners of the tenant farmers who have carried materials . . . Those of Blodwel and Bryn had been here on New Year's Day, and the masons on 30th November of last year. So that now I have, on this account, received seventy-six guests in all'. He had shared his personal success with the parishioners who had helped him.

On Thursday, 14th August, 1856, all the scaffolding had been removed from the tower and the 'appearance of my spire when disencumbered from the scaffolding, was exactly what I wished and expected . . . the convex outline of the spire has, I think, a certain degree of scientific and geometrical grandeur; and it also appears to me far more beautiful than the ordinary form'. It had been a long and difficult undertaking but he was more than satisfied with his spire and it must remain to this day unique in its design. The overall height is 104 feet, the tower being 57 feet and the spire 47 feet.

His commitment to the work had been great. He had designed and supervised its construction on almost a daily basis. The financial cost had also been considerable:

'I have paid for the tower according to my cheque book £1,400, that is £700 for two consecutive years. The carriage of material was mostly given by my parishioners and was probably worth £100 more. Penson saw the tower when half done and told me it would not cost less than £1,600. It is satisfactory to me to be able to show that I have been able to build it under a professional architect's estimate.'

A covered way connects the tower to the church and on the curved archway the following words are inscribed: 'From lightning and Tempest, From earthquake and fire, Good Lord deliver us'.

His problems however, were not yet over! After the completion of the spire, criticisms soon emerged and not only local criticism but in national Journals like 'The Builder'. In this instance a correspondent whom Parker believed to be a local person, had made a vicious and personal attack upon him for undertaking the work. In effect, it was a criticism that an 'amateur' had designed and superintended the whole work. Parker was normally a placid man and not one given to rise to such criticism, but in this instance he considered that the anonymous writer in 'The Builder' had gone too far and he felt that he had to answer and defend himself. His confidence in his own ability to undertake the work was never in any doubt. His full reply and his justification for the work which he did appears in Appendix I.

Immediately after the completion of the spire and the erection of the school and school master's house, and despite his failing health, he became involved with the restoration work that was being carried out at Ludlow church. Here again his expert knowledge of Gothic art was sought by the restorer for the new west window, and their confidence in him was such that his suggestions were put to and agreed, to a large extent, by none other than George Gilbert Scott who was the architect responsible for the restoration work.

On the 13th August, 1860, John Parker died and is buried in the churchyard within a few feet of 'his spire'.

Visitors to the church today may not all appreciate what was done by him, but they will all depart with a feeling of astonishment that it was all done by one man – for undoubtedly the church of St Michael the Archangel, is the creation of John Parker.

Chapter 6

The Botanist

Another of Parker's interests which is worthy of attention was his love of botany. His Journals indicate that he not only had an interest in the subject but that he also possessed considerable knowledge. This was not a passing fancy but something which he nurtured throughout his lifetime, and this interest was augmented after each of his visits to the mountains of Snowdonia. It was here that he encountered the rare alpine plants in their natural habitat, and it was only in their natural habitat that he could appreciate their beauty. For him their habitat was as important as the plants themselves.

Today, most of us are aware of the need and urgency to protect plants and their habitats, but we still tend to take for granted the plant life that we see around us. At the time when the Victorian plant hunters were most active, Parker was already advocating conservation. He could see the dangers that were lurking because of their unending search for plants. It was a matter of much regret to him that so many species had been exterminated by generations of plant collectors, but consolation that others had become restricted to places what could only be reached by expert climbers and therefore safeguarded for the future.

Probably no other area in Britain is more attractive to the botanist than Snowdonia. The flora is rich and varied and the compactness of the area makes it an attractive venue for short excursions which are likely to provide a wide variety of plants. It has long been the haunt of botanists since the days of Thomas Johnson who visited the area in 1639 in the company of Thomas Glynne of Glynllifon near Caernarfon. In 1641 he published the account of his journey under the title 'Mercurii Botanici, or a Description of a Journey Undertaken for the Sake of Plants into Cambria or Wales'.

Edward Lhuyd, a great Welsh scholar, naturalist, archaeologist and traveller, followed in 1682. He was described by Sir Hans Sloan as 'the greatest botanist in Europe'. It was Lhuyd who discovered the Snowdon Lily and it was named 'Lloydia Serotina' after him. This is an inconspicuous single flower of slender stem with white petals with brownish-red veins and yellowish centre and with several thread-like leaves. This plant grows only in about half a dozen locations in Snowdonia and is not found anywhere else in Britain. It was a rare plant in Lhuyd's day but is now much rarer through the depredation of the plant collectors. It does not appear that Parker came across this plant on his tours because there is no mention of it in his Journals although he did go quite often to the Devil's Kitchen, where it was known to be flowering. His tours were arranged at various times of the year so as to observe the area in its various moods and colours and also increase his chances of seeing as many plants as possible in flower.

Another favourite haunt of the plant collectors, including Parker, was Clogwyn Du'r Arddu, on Snowdon, where the Lloydia Serotina was known to grow. He would certainly have been aware of the importance of this particular precipice in mountaineering history. William Bingley in his book *North Wales, including its Scenery, Antiquities and Customs* published in 1804 recalls a particular plant collecting excursion to this cliff in 1798 in the company of the Revd Peter Bayley Williams, Rector of Llanrug and Llanberis, in the following words:

'We had along with us a small basket to contain our provisions and hold roots of such plants as he (Peter Bayley Williams) wished to transfer to his garden, this he carried behind him by means of a leather belt fastened round his waist. When, therefore, he had fixed himself securely to a part of the rock, he took off his belt, and holding firmly by one end, gave the other to me; I laid hold, and with a little aid from the stones, fairly pulled myself up by it.'

This was the first ever recorded rock-climb in Britain.

Parker's ability as an artist was of considerable advantage to him and it was a gift which he made great use of in furtherance of his botanical interest. He had very deep-rooted ideas about how he wanted to paint flowers and his water-colours in the National Library of Wales is adequate proof of this. Whilst acknowledging that unembellished botanical paintings had their place, he showed more interest in painting the flowers in their natural habitat, and from his Journals it would appear that he took considerable care in selecting appropriate sites and materials for such paintings. His small treatise on 'flower landscapes' as he was wont to call them demonstrates his reasoning. It also serves as a valuable aid when looking at his water-colours:

'Rules for the artistic treatment of Botanical Scenery
or
Flower Landscape.

The whole plant represented, and especially the flowers, must be somewhat larger than the actual size. For we see partly round the leaf or flower; viewing it with both eyes and therefore from two points at once, which in a small object magnifies the surface and also modifies the outline. Again, strong light is a great magnifier; the blossoms actually swell into the light, and the image of their form thus presented to the eye, is visibly distended. But no such effect is produced by light on the flat surface of a drawing. Unless the artist therefore enlarges the actual scale of his flower he cannot fairly give the effect of nature. Moreover, the human eye has a tendency to magnify any object on which it gazes with special interest or attention.

The treatment of a botanical background is more difficult than that of the main subject. In the beginning of the present century, some large coloured engravings were published in which the backgrounds were sometimes distant mountains, or large buildings, and in general a great extent of sky was represented. The experiment was unsuccessful. It was an erroneous conception. The human eye, probably never sees at the same instant a flower near enough to show itself completely and a range of hills miles off, or buildings of any magnitude. When we contemplate a group of wild flowers we see little else than the immediate accidents of their locality. We see the moss, the stone, the sticks, or maybe, the crawling insect, and beyond these a dim shadowy mottling of purple and green and brown indicates the field or the hedge close by – the real horizon of our flower landscape.

Yet, within these confined limits, what prodigies of colour and form are displayed! Within the compass of half a dozen yards or feet, you have specimens of the same plant in the foreground or in distance, in light or in shade, in bud or in bloom, and all varieties of position in their different ways exhibiting the properties of that figure which the plant assumes for itself. In the selection of appropriate accompaniments, and the grouping of the main subject, there is perhaps as much art required as in the composition of the largest landscape. You look upon a bank of snowdrops or daffodils and unless you see them with the eye of a practised artist, they will appear to be all of the same size. But examine more closely the floral picture and the means by which the brilliant effect of it is produced. The nearest flowers are full size. Those which are further off are only half size. Those which are furthest off are mere dots. That is their visual appearance, and if you do not represent them so, you violate the laws of perspective. If you do not give the due gradation of distance, you commit the same fault as the would-be-artist, who, because he knows that mountains are large, makes them larger than his nearest foreground.

The whole extent of a botanical scene or flower landscape is contained in the foreground of a general or ordinary view. The actual sky will seldom appear, for flowers are usually somewhat below the eye.

Having fixed upon general arrangement of your flower landscape, you must carefully select, from different spots, the individual flowers best adapted for your purpose. It will never do to take them at random, or bind yourself down to represent each flower in the very place and attitude of its growth. Nature in her best mood, is beyond the reach of imitation by an artist. But nature in her ordinary mood, may be surpassed by the skilful combination of art.'

What he wrote in that treatise is what he practised in his flower landscapes, and he took great care in the selection of his subjects. In May, 1856, he wrote to his niece Fanny, giving her an account of a large flower landscape of the Wood-sorrel (Oxalis acetosella) that he was working on. It was represented as growing in a deep glen near his home. It was screened from every wind, and he sat for two hours collecting materials for his drawing. 'It was the only day in the whole year when those materials could be collected. I have been there since – the blossoms are become seeds – the dead leaves are blown away, the coarse grasses are growing up, the cascade has lost its mossy gloom, and all the romance of colouring has disappeared.' This was the meticulous artist at his best and always striving for perfection.

Parker's detailed notes for his illustration of the Wood sorrel:

'The habitat of the Wood sorrel (Oxalis acetosella).

The time of year selected for this flower landscape is before the middle of May, during a period of several days without rain. On a stone lying on one side of a small rill at the bottom of a deep and winding dell, is represented a group of the common Wood sorrel, in blossom, subdivided by dry leaves of oak and maple, and rising from a cushion of moss, interspersed with golden saxifrage (Chrysosplenium oppositifolium), pilewort or lesser celandine, strawberry leaves, and Herb Robert. The leaf of this plant (Geranium Robertoanum), is in spring frequently seen of a deep red. The shallow scanty pool is crossed by long branches, and in it the stems of trees above, not seen in the drawing, are reflected. Beyond it is a bank of shale rock, smothered in moss, down which the trickling moisture of a stream, nearly dry, produces a miniature cascade. There is no spray or froth, if indeed there had been, it would have interfered with the main subject of the foreground. This effect rarely continues for more than one day: the water silent, and almost without motion, looks, in the place itself, more like a drawing than reality. The sides of the dell are very steep, covered with moss, trailing ivy, withered leaves and ferns. On the right side are overhanging stones, and above the cascade is another leaning stone, lying apart. No sky is to be seen, but the view is closed by the dell itself, winding in another direction. The style of the whole spot, though very small in scale, indicates a romantic neighbourhood.'

Chapter 7

A Tour in North Wales

North Wales with its varied scenery of mountains and coastline, rivers and lakes was the natural haunts of the early travellers. But regardless of this, why did they all come to Wales and what did they expect to find here?

It had long been the practice for the sons of the landed gentry in England to spend a year or two in travelling through Europe on the 'Grand Tour' so as to complete their education. It constituted a significant interlude in their early years.

By the end of the eighteenth century and the beginning of the nineteenth century conditions for travelling through Europe were far from satisfactory because of the numerous wars that were in progress. This situation reached its zenith with the French Revolution (1789-1798) and the war between England and France which ended in 1815. It was not safe, therefore, to travel through the continent as they had been used to, but this did not curtail in any way their desire for travel. There was only one alternative for them and that was to turn their attention much nearer home – to that foreign land that was right on their doorstep with its strange culture and customs and even stranger language.

To all intent and purposes, these early travellers had no knowledge of Wales at all, and yet they did not consider that to be any disadvantage whatsoever as many of their books demonstrate. All that they were concerned with was that the political situation in Europe enabled them to observe how their neighbours lived, and this signalled the emergence of the golden age of the travellers.

They found, however, that in the hinterland of Caernarfonshire, for example, the people were well aware of what was going on in Europe and the French Revolution was very real to them; it coloured the reception which they gave to strangers who came into their midst.

When Edward Pugh, the traveller and artist from Ruthin toured Wales at the beginning of the nineteenth century collecting material for his book 'Cambria Depicta' he often came face to face with the problem. Once, when he tried to get accommodation at a Public House at Llanllyfni, a few miles outside Caernarfon, he received a very cold welcome. The publican's son opened the door and shouted to his father that there was a stranger there asking for accommodation. The father called back 'Is he a Welshman, an Englishman or a Frenchman?' His son answered that he thought he was a Frenchman to which his father replied that he could not stay at his house. This is how Edward Pugh recorded the rest of the incident:

'this man, though unable to speak English, perceived, I believe, that my dialect was not foreign, with a great deal of suspicion, however he viewed me from head to foot. I then in English requested some refreshments, and repeated this request, but received no answer. Finding that my English was not likely to procure for me the comforts of the house I thought it more prudent to alter my mode of proceeding. I went, therefore, to the kitchen, into the midst of the people, who by this time had crowded in, and after some silence on my part, finding myself the subject of their conversation, and that the general opinion was rather unfavourable to me principally on account of my portfolio, I suddenly turned round and replied with some severity in their own language, to an observation which one of them had made. It was not a little laughable to see the alteration in the people's looks at this moment, they instantly left the house, expressing satisfaction on finding that I was not likely to be a spy . . . This part of Wales is very little known to the travellers and the native poor are without means of attaining even a superficial knowledge of the English tongue . . . From these circumstances, they become from principle, jealous of travellers, and especially artists, who are seen (as they term it) lurking about the mountains making maps of the country etc. This jealousy of strangers is by no means peculiar to this part of the country.'

The Reverend Richard Warner also had a similar experience when he was at Llantwit Major, Glamorganshire, on his second walk through Wales in 1798. There was a rumour that a stranger had been sighted in the district who could well have been a spy and about eighty men, women and children had been rounded up to look for him. And later, on his journey from Aberystwyth to Machynlleth, he was mistaken for an escaped prisoner by a cottager. Warner had become lost on his journey – an usual occurrence when maps were so scarce and unreliable. This mistrust of foreigners remained in country districts for a long time.

The French Revolution did certainly cast its shadow over Wales during this period and contributed to the influx of travellers, but it was not the only reason. This was also the period when the Industrial Revolution was at its peak and created a wealthy middle class. This new middle class was also anxious to imitate the gentry and Wales provided a quick and convenient foreign land for them to travel to.

Whilst there had been a considerable improvement in the condition of the roads, serious problems still remained particularly so in outlying country districts where the roads had not been improved.

In her book *Glimpses of Welsh Life and Character*, Marie Trevelyan refers to this particular problem:

'In out of the way places it was nothing to meet half a dozen men carrying their wives pick-a-back to or from chapel, when the roads were in a very terrible condition.'

This, therefore, was the situation in Wales when Parker started his journals with a visit he made in September, 1819 when still a student at Oxford. He had made earlier visits whilst a school boy at Eton and had also visited his uncle who lived at Bodowen, Barmouth.

The literary output of other travellers often contain long passages on Welsh history – and frequently incorrect, but Parker desists from this although he was aware of the important chapters in the history of Wales, and this becomes apparent when he writes about his visits to such historically important sites as the Abbeys of Cwm Hir, Tintern, Valle Crucis and Ystrad Fflur. He was in his element when discussing these because he could combine his interest in Gothic art with history and church history in particular. His journals however, are full of detailed descriptions of the landscape as he journeys back and forth through the mountains of Snowdonia.

Reference has already been made to the problems of travel in Wales in these early years and Parker himself had an experience which could well have ended in disaster.

On 1st October, 1819 he and his friend arrived at Ffestiniog having first visited a local beauty spot called Pulpud Hugh Llwyd and after feasting on ale and cheese and the best bread they had ever tasted, they returned through the Vale of Ffestiniog admiring the great beauty of the landscape.

The following morning his friend went ahead of him on horseback, and before breakfast Parker went up the vale to a meadow by the River Dwyryd where he bathed. He found the water a brilliant chestnut colour and very cold. After breakfast he followed his friend and walked to Beddgelert where he arrived at three o'clock. It had been their intention to proceed to Llanberis that night but decided against it.

He was up at seven the following morning to make a drawing of the church. The summit of Moel Hebog was wreathed with beautiful rose coloured clouds throwing a deep violet shade upon some fine precipices. (These colours predominated his water colours of mountain scenery.)

Having hired a pony he went past Dinas Emrys and Llyn Dinas, Llyn Gwynant and Cwm Dyli, and:

'Trusting to my knowledge of the mountains, rode out of the Capel Curig road intending to gain a pathway to Llanberis, but this, though seen from the road for some distance, is obliterated before it reaches it, and scientific mountaineers are the only safe conductors, for I was riding through rather boggy ground. My pony stopped short, I whipped him on, but in an instance I found him sinking under me in a green morass. I leapt off and reached the other side for it was not many feet wide, and lugged out the poor pony struggling with his terror and accusing me with his eyes in quite a worrying manner. We were at last on the other side minus a stirrup and a glove which may reward antiquarian researchers when this morass is explored.'

This was an early escapade from which he must have benefited for he does not record any other similar incident in his forty years of travelling through North Wales.

Within nine months he was back in Snowdonia again with the intention of climbing Snowdon at night so as to witness the sun rise. Late in the evening he and his friend Neave left Beddgelert on their ponies. It was a warm night and the moonlight was already fading when they arrived at Snowdon Cottage on the shores of Llyn Cwellyn, Rhyd-ddu, where the guide lived. After a short climb, the path which they took was too steep for the ponies to ascend so they dismounted and continued on foot. The boy who accompanied them was sent down the path leading to Llanberis and they continued on the path which would eventually lead them to the summit of Snowdon. When they were within a quarter of a mile from the summit:

'The sun broke forth upon our left hand immediately shedding a glow of rose coloured light upon the chief summit only. We stood for a few seconds to admire some patches of the Snowdon Pink (Silene acaulis) in full blossom. The disk of the sun as he was rising was reflected in the sea with a dark line between his orb and the reflection.

We enjoyed this grand prospect for about an hour, and then finding ourselves in want of sleep, lay down beneath the chief summit. We were soon visited by several shepherds and boys who

47

were watching the progress of a pack of foxhounds (ten couples) along Bwlch y Saethau. Some shepherds were following them and others contemplating the scene from a more distant situation.'

They came down from the summit and by Ffynnon Frech (Llyn Bach) they consumed their provisions and slept in the sun. Having recovered sufficiently they continued their descent to the Pass of Llanberis 'considered to be one of the finest things of its kind in the world' and walked up the Pass to Gorphwysfa and then descended through Cwm Dyli and reached Beddgelert fatigued at twilight.

By the following morning they were adequately refreshed and took the chaise to Caernarfon and stayed at the Goat Inn which was situated at The Green (Castle Square today). They sent for Richard Davies, a blind harpist to entertain them and Parker was full of admiration for this gentleman 'he played the Overture from Sampson almost all through without more than a trifling deviation from the very notes of the original'. A letter from Parker to his niece Fanny suggests that he had an interest and knowledge of music.

In his room at the Goat Inn there was a book for the benefit of travellers entitled 'Letters from Snowdon' by Joseph Craddock and published in 1770. Parker was not very impressed with this little book because:

'is comprises a greater number of falsehoods and inconsistencies than I would have expected to find in so small a publication. Amongst other instances of inaccuracies the author passes within half a mile of the small lake of Llyn y Dywarchen on which there is a very curious floating island rendered still more so from its having been mentioned by Giraldus many centuries ago. The sagacious tourist however not only denies the present existence of it but ridicules Giraldus for its fabulous invention.'

On his way to Caernarfon, Parker had visited this particular lake in the Nantlle Valley a few miles outside Caernarfon and had made a drawing of it.

Thomas Pennant also mentions this lake with its peculiar island in his *Tours of Wales* as does Edward Pugh in his *Cambria Depicta*. Pugh describes the island as being:

'probably eight yards in length and four or five across. The people here say it is a certain prognostic of fair or foul weather as it floats to the one or other end of the pool. A boy who lives close by, amuses himself by swimming to it, and, taking the helm, he steers it to any part of the pool he pleases.'

This particular tour to North Wales lasted just twelve days, and Parker ends his journal with the following words:

'Frequently as I have been in Wales, this last tour has left a more splendid impression upon my fancy than any other, the almost uninterrupted clearness of the weather, the fortunate time of year and the freedom from embarrassment as to an university examination, all contributed to render it delightful. Upon looking back upon the last twelve days, I can hardly describe the pleasing confusion of ideas and recollections that arise. All these considerations induce us to ask the question where else could our time have been employed more pleasingly or where with more advantage or more profit?'

These were sentiments he was to express many times during the next forty years of travelling in Wales.

Chapter 8

Welsh Hospitality

The first books on travels through Wales which we have are the works of Giraldus Cambrensis when he toured the country in 1188 in the company of Archbishop Baldwin preaching and recruiting men for the Crusades. Baldwin could not have had a better guide and we are fortunate that it was Giraldus who accompanied him because he was a great literary figure who had an interest in the history of Wales. The journey resulted in the two earliest books of tours through Wales i.e. 'Itinerarium Kambriae' (The Journey Through Wales) and 'Descripto Kambriae' (The Description of Wales). In his 'Description of Wales' he writes:

> 'In Wales no one begs. Everyone's home is open to all, for the Welsh generosity and hospitality are the greatest of all virtues. They very much enjoy welcoming others to their homes. When you travel there is no question of you asking for accommodation or of their offering it: you just march into a house and hand over your weapons to the person in charge. They give you water so that you may wash your feet and that means that you are a guest. With these people the offering of water in which to wash one's feet is an invitation to stay. If you refuse the offer, it means that you have only dropped in for refreshment during the early part of the day and that you do not propose to stay the night.'

That was obviously the situation in 1188, but reading through many of the published and unpublished works on Welsh tours it would appear that many of the early travellers expected the situation to have remained the same!

Sir Robert Kerr Porter, did not feel that he had received the welcome to which he thought he was entitled to when he came to Wales in 1799. When he and two of his friends were returning from the summit of Snowdon they came across an isolated cottage which they entered in expectation of a meal. His only comments were that 'at the foot of this rugged length stands a small Hovel or Human Sty where we, in consort with the civil Mr Goodman, contrived to eat egg, bacon and black bread, our moisture was milk and water. Our attendant was skin and bones, aged and civil. She looked as if the world afforded her not the common occurrence of existence'. The party proceeded to Beddgelert where 'we could get no supper for the double-souled Methodist Preacher who drew the bowels of the Welsh village about him in an adjoining mansion for the purpose of saving their consciences from being made the devil's looking glasses'. His Journal is full of such remarks but nowhere does he mention that he had offered to pay for any meals.

Another traveller who thought that things had not changed since the days of Giraldus was C.F. Cliffe. When he and a friend were travelling through Cardiganshire in the 1840's they, like Porter, came across a solitary farmhouse which they entered in search of food. It was a miserable and primitive dwelling with smoke from the turf fire filling the room. They received a warm welcome nevertheless and shared the bread, butter and cheese which was offered together with a quantity of excellent home-brewed beer. As they left they thanked the family for their hospitality, but 'as we were passing out of the house, one of the sons came to us and made a demand for one shilling and a half, in Welsh. The charge was moderate enough, but we felt hurt and surprised at the demand so contrary to the time-honoured observance of Cambrian hospitality; however, we pocketed the affront without any observations'. It seems that these particular travellers thought that the state of affairs described by Giraldus in 1188 still prevailed in Cardiganshire in the 1840's!

When reading through the very detailed Journals of John Parker I find it regrettable that there are so few references in them to the people whom he met on his journeys and their reaction to him, since such an account would be very illuminating today. But nowhere does he complain about the welcome which he received.

In July, 1833, he was to enjoy the sort of welcome and hospitality referred to by Giraldus! He had been sketching on the shores of Lake Eigiau above Capel Curig, and after:

'making a sketch of the lake, I was invited into the cottage which formed my foreground and is called Hafod y Rhiw. The wind had been dreadfully cold and violent, indeed, I dreaded returning to Capel Curig over the mountain from apprehension of some accident or catching a cold. The mistress of this cottage busied herself in preparing a meal and in lighting a peat fire to dry my shoes. A glass of rum was produced and another poured into a basin of warm milk and sugar.

51

A large oatmeal cake made its appearance with butter and cwrw (beer) and some cakes were boiled on the hearth. The good lady was also getting ready some tea (black and green) which however I declined, in short there was no lack of provisions or welcome at this cottage. Had it not been for this timely refreshment, I should probably have caught a dangerous cold for not having intended when I left Capel Curig to go so far. I had no spirits to mix with water at the mountain torrents and had only a dry luncheon of egg sandwich. At half past five I left this house of entertainment and partly from not having smaller silver and partly from a wish to reward attention to a lonely tourist, I gave her two shillings. The gale still blew violently much to my discomfort . . . The clouds covered all the mountains as I trudged along through rocks and bogs for two miles till I descended into the Irish Road. The Mail passed me at 8 o'clock and I reached Capel Curig soon after wet through in my feet but otherwise none the worse for my day's labour'.

And Parker, nearly seven hundred years after Giraldus, had experienced 'Welsh generosity and hospitality . . . the greatest of all virtues'.

Chapter 9

The Churches of Wales I

The plight of the churches in Wales was of considerable interest to the early travellers and this is not surprising since so many of them were clergymen.

In 1774, Henry Penruddock Wyndham made a tour of Wales and in Pembrokeshire he went in search of St David's Cathedral and found:

'A street of miserable cottages one of which is the Inn comprises the city of St David's. I had so little notion of it being the bishopric that I enquired in the street how far it was to St David's . . . The whole church is in a very dirty and slovenly condition, part of it is not paved, and the graves are raised within it, in the same manner as in common churches. There is something simple and pleasing in the idea of strewing flowers and evergreen over the grave of a departed friend, which is the universal custom in these parts. But when we saw the faded plants rotting on new raised earth within the walls of the church it became offensive and disgusting.'

Undoubtedly, one of the most distinguished literary figures who toured Wales was Dr Samuel Johnson who, also in 1774 was on a tour of North Wales in the company of his close friend Mrs Hester Lynch Thrale. In the Llŷn Peninsula they visited the churches of Tudweiliog and Llangwnnadl where Dr Johnson remarked:

'We surveyed the churches, which are man and neglected to a degree scarcely imaginable – they have no pavements, and the earth in full of holes – one of them has a breach in the roof – On the desk, I think, of each lay a folio Welsh Bible of the Black Letter, which the curate cannot easily read.'

Remarks similar to these were almost the universal comments of the early travellers. Very few church were considered worthy of praise.

Some travellers thought that one of the reasons for this was the rapid promulgation of Methodism throughout the country. At Haverfordwest,

Wyndham witnessed:

' . . . in the most retired spots of this country, a wretched cottage nearly bursting with the fullness of its congregation; while multitudes, in a heavy rain were swarming about outside, imbibing, with gaping mouths, the poisonous tenets of the preacher.'

This was a situation which few of the early travellers could comprehend and they showed no inclination to understand it. But was this a prejudicial view which they held? Apparently not.

The Welshman Robert Roberts (the Wandering Scholar) described a journey in Anglesey. He had just passed Llannerch-y-medd when he noticed a small church by the wayside, and on entering he observed:

'The oak seats were slowly rotting to pieces, the font was dismantled, and had only a broken pedestal remaining. The altar had no covering of any sort to hide the nakedness of its moth-eaten wood, and the rails were all awry and loose. I thought at first that the church was entirely abandoned to the bats, but the sight of a damp, dingy, ragged surplice hanging over the reading desk showed that some attempt at a service was still made.'

By the time John Parker was travelling it had been recognized that something had to be done to improve the fabric of the churches if only in an attempt to stem the growth of Methodism by making the churches more comfortable and enticing for the congregation.

By the middle of the 1820's many churches were in the process of being renovated, but unfortunately the improvements that were instigated took little notice of the architectural and historical importance of the treasures which many of the country churches possessed. The result was that many of the churches were ruined and their most beautiful treasures lost forever.

But for the fact that Parker was travelling through Wales just before the 'great official vandalism' took place and that he had visited all the churches which contained any vestige of Gothic art and recorded them in great detail in his architectural drawings we would know nothing of the treasures which have been lost. There was no other person undertaking this task at the time and recording for posterity the riches which these ancient churches contained. This is justification enough for the debt which is owed to him.

From an architectural point of view, the late fifteenth and early sixteenth century was the period which gave the churches in Wales a more elaborate character than before. After a period of nearly three centuries of almost fatal inactivity, the ecclesiastical authorities were beginning to display a more energetic desire to restore the churches. They had realized that the people of Wales had been alienated in their affections from the church, and that a great number of churches had been allowed to approximate very closely the condition of any poor farmhouse. Churches of outstanding historical importance and architectural excellence had been abandoned. Parker himself referred to them as 'barns'.

One writer in 1846 wrote:

'We have seen churches so damp and dirty that no gentleman would allow his kitchen to be kept in the same state: the earthen floors worn into pairs of deep holes by the feet of the rustic occupiers of seats during successive generations; the communion table, small and rickety, covered or rather uncovered by a moth-eaten mouldy cloth; the population of the parish five hundred, the congregation fifty; hard by the church, the rectory, a spacious, comfortable well-furnished dwelling; and not many furlongs off, a large staring and ugly meeting-house with its double range of windows and low pitched roof, well floored, well glazed, well lighted, well warmed, well cleaned, and not only well frequented, but inside full, galleries and all, and the people thronging the doorways – and that not on Sundays alone, but on other days also.'

This was not something that could be allowed to continue unchecked and something had to be done to safeguard the status and influence of the church.

There was a slight but discernible change in attitude towards church architecture and a desire for the return of Gothic styles and principles. This was something that Parker would have approved of; he longed for the return of such style and this would have been uppermost in his mind when he visited the remote churches to record their Gothic screens and fonts, bosses and windows. Not only have his meticulous and painstaking architectural drawings been an invaluable record of such treasures of Gothic art but they have also been used as a basis for the reconstruction of screens as at Llangurig where the original screen, drawn by him, had been removed and destroyed.

Parker's diligent work in recording the church screens of Wales has given us an understanding of the work of mediaeval craftsmen that would otherwise have been lost by the work of indifferent restorers. His uncompromising views on all things Gothic remained with him throughout his life and the knowledge which he had gleaned he put into good use when restoring his own churches at Llanmerewig and Llanyblodwel and in the building of the church at Oswestry. His enthusiasm knew no bounds, and he would travel anywhere to further his knowledge and this is quite obvious from his writings when he compares the intricacies of one screen with another, knowledge which he could only have acquired from a detailed study of the actual screens.

He was quite convinced after studying Gothic architecture on the continent that the triumphant progress of Gothic art 'was cut short by papal jealousy'. To him:

> 'The art of Gothic is superior both in practice and design. I doubt not, but that the inventors of it, whosoever they were, entertained a latent hatred of Rome, her style, her system and above all her mode of building. An architectural secret was discovered that shook the pre-eminence of Rome in this art. The discovery was combined with an expression of solemn and earnest feeling such as the Scriptures could only supply. The inventor of Gothic was to art what the Reformation was to the Christian Religion.'

This appears to have been his attitude towards Gothic architecture throughout his life and he never wavered from it. In a treatise he wrote on the construction and improvement of churches he felt that the object of the Roman Catholic ceremonial was to strike the imagination more than to satisfy the mind, but that the Church of England avowed to the latter as to the chief use of public worship. The buildings designed respectively by these two different modes of religion would assume a corresponding difference of character, and the Gothic style was the obvious choice for the Church of England. This was also confirmed later by A.W. Pugin who was converted to the notion that Gothic was the only possible architecture for a true Christian church.

The lethargy which the church had fallen into during the eighteenth century resulted in the establishment of the Oxford Movement in 1833 whose members wanted to see a revival of the church ritual and ceremonies which had fallen into disuse since the Reformation. In this respect, Parker could not be called a Tractarian as he did not agree with the demarcation of the Clergy and the congregation by altar rails and screens, and like other Clergy he would have been outraged by any return of 'Romanism'.

Although a number of screens were lost during reconstruction works, he agreed that they were encumbrances to a Protestant place of worship, for they had a tendency to prevent the communion service being performed at the altar, but they should not have been destroyed. In general they contained carved work of great elegance. If their removal was absolutely necessary he maintained that the work should only be carried out under the guidance of a 'Gothic architect' who might be able to transform them into organ lofts without damage to the fine Gothic woodwork – 'the fancy dwells with a pleasing wonder on the florid and varied workmanship that is displayed in it; and when you turn to the meagre stiffness of modern pews, wholly destitute of taste or ornament, you cannot help wondering that, in this respect we should have so strangely declined from the fine models of the darker ages.'

These details and ornaments were an inspiration to him when restoring the churches at Llanmerewig and Llanyblodwel where he was able to put his thoughts and ideas into action and reaffirm his strong views on Gothic architecture. His vast experience of Welsh chancel screens led him to the opinion that in point of decoration they would never be surpassed.

He expressed the belief more than once, that the restoration of churches should not be left to 'mere builders' a view which was expressed very forcibly by George Gilbert Scott (1811-1878), the architect responsible for the restoration in Wales of St David's, Bangor and St Asaph Cathedrals, who in his *Personal and Professional Recollections* wrote:

'The country has been, and continues to be, actually devastated with destruction under the name of restoration. For years and years the vast majority of the churches to be restored have been committed to men who neither know nor care anything whatever about them, and out of whose hands they have emerged in a condition truly deplorable, stripped of almost everything which gave them interest or value.'

This was the experience which Parker knew only too well from his visits to the churches of Wales.

Chapter 10

The Churches of Wales II

In North and mid-Wales, where Parker had the most intimate knowledge, it is not surprising that the parish churches were located in the most inhospitable locations and that many of them were not directly sited within a village community, but rather in a central position so as to be reasonably accessible to the majority of the parishioners.

They were often located on a prominent site, often on a hillock and were frequently white-washed so as to be clearly seen and also for protection because lime-wash was considered a good preservative. The roads leading up to them were nothing more than tracks and yet, as Parker so often pointed out, many of those remote barn-like buildings contained outstanding and ancient treasures in the form of finely carved chancel screens.

In construction they were usually rectangular, without aisles and having a stone tower or timber belfry, and a cursory look through the various 'Tours of Wales' by the early travellers will reveal that they were generally in a deplorable condition. Many became the abode of bats, but surprisingly enough, Parker did at one time advocate the introduction of a small colony into his church in the hope that they would keep down the mice and the spiders!

When the time came that some form of repairs had to be undertaken to prevent the complete collapse of these remote churches, such repairs more often than not, resulted in the complete destruction of many of their important features. The idea that 'new was beautiful' was very hard to dispel.

Not all the churches, however, were just victims of neglect, some were targets of wanton vandalism. The Ven. Archdeacon de Winton removed the roof of both his churches at Cefnllys and Llandrindod, Radnorshire so as to ensure their destruction. The furniture was left to be destroyed by the elements. His reason for such malicious destruction was to save the expense of a Curate and to force the congregation of the two parishes to walk two and a half miles to the new church at

Llandrindod. The Archdeacon's house stood within a few yards of his new church. The altar rails from Cefnllys were used to close up a gap in a farm hedge to stop animals from straying.

When all this is taken into consideration, it cannot be anything other than surprising that so many of the masterpieces of woodwork which the churches contained have been preserved for us today. They are our heritage and we have a responsibility to maintain them and safeguard them for future generations to enjoy. This was certainly the view expressed by Parker when he wrote in his Journal:

' . . . while in unfrequented solitude we find that some hand of no ordinary power has left a record of ingenious talent well worth rescuing from oblivion. The running patterns of stem and foliage of which the cornices of these chancel screens are composed, are done to a degree of spirit and industry that renders their competition almost hopeless. Nothing rivals them but the carved flower work of Gibbons.'

If the above was true in Parker's days how much more important it is today when so many of these ancient churches are unfortunately closing and being sold off.

Large numbers of screens have disappeared or have been altered since the middle of the eighteenth century, and their former existence is only validated by reference to old Vestry Books and by Parker's dedication in providing us with such wealth of meticulous and accurate drawings.

Chancel and Rood Screens

It was his consuming passion in Gothic architecture, and screens in particular, which led him to the churches of Wales. We do not have any direct evidence as to the welcome he would have received from some of his fellow clergymen who found him spending considerable time in their churches with his measuring tape and artist's materials, but we do know that when he visited the church at Clarach, Cardiganshire, he wrote in his Journal that he spoke to the master-mason who was working on the church at the time 'and gave him some architectural advice'. But nothing would have discouraged him from his study of the screens.

The 'Rood Screen' was that which separated the choir or chancel from the nave of the church. It was erected in conjunction with the rood, which in Old English meant 'cross' or 'crucifix'. Originally the rood was supported on a single beam spanning the nave at the entrance to the chancel. Later a rood screen was added, rising from the floor to the beam and a rood loft was also sometimes added. It was upon this loft that the rood was displayed together with the statues of the Virgin Mary and St John. The loft became known as the singing gallery because it was here on certain feast days that the minstrels performed.

From the fourteenth century until the sixteenth century rood screens and lofts were prominent features of church furniture and they provided artists with an opportunity to display their skills in the creation of elaborate carvings and paintings.

Upon the dissolution of the monasteries and the establishment of the Anglican church by Henry VIII, he decreed that the rood and everything else above the rood beam should be removed, but the rood screen could be retained and it then became known as the chancel screen. As a result of this many rood lofts were removed but there was a reluctance to conform in some parts of Wales and a great number of lofts were retained as singing galleries. It could well be said the love of music was the contributing factor in saving so many of our rood lofts. But as choirs became augmented by the addition of musicians and their instruments, the galleries housed more people than they were intended to and some became unsafe. The reluctance to effect any repairs meant that many of the screens and lofts were allowed to deteriorate beyond repair.

The position remained unsatisfactory until as late as 1851 when the Incorporated Church Building Society reported that 'many of the churches in Wales are in a much more dilapidated condition than any in England'. Parker, however, often referred to the injudicious repairs that had been carried out and the complete indifference to carved woodwork which aggravated the situation. He had witnessed the complete demolition of screens in the name of restoration and some which had become fringe benefits for the contractors or fuel for poor parishioners.

As some screens contained painted panels of saints, whose very presence were later considered as superstitious and defamatory, their removal was unconstrained. The screen at Old Radnor was described in 1818 as 'a beautiful screen that divides the nave from the chancel, most richly carved in oak, painted, gilded and bearing on it representations of saints and religious persons, placed in ranges, compartments or niches . . . it extends entirely across the nave and the two lateral sides'. These paintings were subsequently removed.

Parker's detailed notes and careful drawings of some of the screens are worthy of attention. He did not have to travel far to see some of the most outstanding examples in Wales.

(i) St Mary, Newtown, Montgomeryshire

When Richard Fenton visited Newtown in 1810 he was impressed with the screen at Newtown and wrote: 'The rood loft, as to carving, gilding and painting is perhaps the most perfect thing of its kind in the kingdom; said to have come from Abbey Cwm Hir. There are no two compartments alike.'

Parker visited this church on a number of occasions, the first in 1829, and like Fenton before him thought that the screen had been brought from the Abbey of Cwm Hir – this view is not now accepted. His first observations were:

'The chancel screen which at present adorns the church at Newtown, is one of gorgeous remnants of monastic antiquity which leaves no hope to the modern artist of excelling in rich ornaments his ancient models . . . That such a mass of delicate and highly wrought work should have been preserved at all is fortunate and extraordinary, but the present remains in Newtown church are in a sorry state of sad disorder that they convey no notion whatever of the general effect in its original situation.'

There had obviously been a great deal of deterioration since Fenton's visit but despite the fact that the screen was in a ruinous condition, Parker could see that the fragments themselves revealed a wealth of Gothic art of original and exquisite patterns which, when it was complete would have presented 'the spectator with the highest luxuries of workmanship and colouring'.

He had confronted specimens of rich carvings in other screens, but at Newtown he found:

'A specimen of ancient colouring by which the rules may be discovered for this rare branch of Gothic art. The skilful contrasting of blue and red, of purple and gold upon a dark brown ground are here displayed. The method of preserving the spirit and effect of carving when gilt and coloured, are to be observed here, and the general effect which this colouring produced, was I think a dreamy, shadowy brightness combined with most elaborate workmanship.'

He made subsequent visits in June, 1830 and October, 1832, to prepare a more detailed account of the screen and these visits culminated in a number of drawings of various sections, but it does not appear that he made a drawing of the complete screen. He notes, however,

'The centre of this gorgeous fabric, that part which combined the chief entrance, has been altogether destroyed . . . My object therefore is to present a restoration of one of these interior entrances, the larger one being no longer in existence. The general disposition of parts admits of no question of dispute.'

In all he prepared at least 12 drawing of the screen but as every part of it was in a state of disorder, he selected from various parts those patterns which appeared most elegant.

Although the screen was damaged when he first saw it in 1829 it has suffered further damage. A new church was erected in 1847 and the screen was removed there with parts being stored in the rectory. In 1942 the Revd Canon J.E. Morgan reported that when he was appointed Rector, parts of its were scattered about the stable loft. Parts of the screen were also stripped of their colour when they were used for panelling the sanctuary. But Parker's carefully coloured drawings have survived.

(ii) St Gwynog, Llanwnog, Montgomeryshire.

This was another church which was to receive many visits by Parker because of its outstanding chancel screen. His first visit was in 1828 when he described it as being 'tolerably perfect'. He was later to describe it as:

'This gem of Gothic woodwork is as nearly perfect in design as anything that we know of. It would be difficult for us to suggest any alterations that would not be injurious. Never have we met with the variety, lightness, elegance and regularity so successfully combined as in this beautiful screen. It is a remarkably fine specimen of Gothic woodwork in a style very different from what is met with elsewhere.'

The church itself is an unpretentious building typical of so many Welsh country churches and one which had been left to deteriorate to such an extent that in 1863 it was heavily restored. From subsequent reports it would seem that the screen has also been altered to some extent from what it was in Parker's day, but nevertheless, it is still an exquisite gem of Gothic work as described by him.

(iii) St Monacella, Pennant Melangell, Montgomeryshire.

In a remote valley amongst the hills behind Llangynog and forming perhaps one of the most beautiful and romantic spots in the country, lies the little church of St Monacella (Melangell in Welsh). The picturesque location of the church itself was enough to attract Parker to it, but in the church he found an unique screen with its oak carving depicting the legend of St Monacella. This screen has also been modified since he visited it and his description of it is, therefore, all the more interesting:

'Within this branch of work of a running border, such as is frequent in chancel screens, and enclosed in casement mouldings, the legend of St Melangell is represented. The cleverness and ingenuity with which the story is told, in spite of the trammels imposed upon the artist by the requirements of the running border, are deserving of remarks.

The various figures, although carved in equally strong relief, and occupying equal intervals of the branch work and foliage in a running border, are nevertheless at five several distances in point of size. There is no grouping, the workmanship is minute, but rather grotesque; and the different animals are all more or less, out of drawing. They are painted red and pink and white, the tracery panels under them, alternately red and blue; the leading members of some pale colour. The branch work and the foliage are also of light colours, but the chromatic decorations are much faded, and there is not light enough to ascertain them. One tracery panel has its gouge work painted red, the next blue, that of the next red, and so on alternately. The screen itself, on the rood loft of which the above formed a cornice or frieze, still remains in its position between the chancel and the nave. It comprises four compartments on each side of the doorway, or entrance, which is just double the width of the side divisions; the spandrels are filled with tracery of the same design and are of 14th century character. Scenes on the border trail are: (1) Brochwel Yscythrog, Prince of Powys on horseback with a sword in his right hand; (2) Half kneeling huntsman trying in vain to remove the horn which he was raising to his lips for the purpose of blowing it, when it remained fast and could not be sounded; (3) St Melangell represented as an Abbess on a cushion, her left hand grasping a foliated crosier; (4) The hunted hare scuttling towards the figure of the Saint. The hare is painted red; (5) A greyhound in pursuit with its leg entangled among the branches of the running border. The dog is painted of a pale colour; (6) A nondescript animal, intended, I suppose for a dog.'

According to the legend, King Brochwel Yscythrog was hunting in the Vale of Tanat when his hounds raised a hare. He and his huntsmen followed in hot pursuit and when in the narrow valley of Pennant the hare disappeared into thick bushes and was followed by the dogs. When the King found them, he saw to his surprise a beautiful girl kneeling in prayer and the hare lying within the folds of her garments. Unperturbed, the King urged on his dogs but without success. When his huntsman tried to blow his horn it became stuck to his lips and he was unable to blow it. The King realized that the girl was no ordinary person and he asked her what her name was and how long she had lived there. The maiden replied that her name was Monacella and that she was the daughter of King Iochwel of Ireland and that she had fled from her home rather than marry the man whom had been chosen for her by her father. She accordingly came to the Berwyn mountains, lived in a cave under God's protection and passing her days in prayer and meditation. King Brochwel was so impressed with her beauty and concerned for her safety, that he gave her the land adjoining her cell commanding that it should be a sanctuary which no man should violate at pain of death. It was here that Monacella lived for the rest of her life amid the peace and tranquillity of the Pennant valley. The hares became her friends and followed her everywhere like lambs. Monacella also established a small nunnery for virgins who devoted themselves entirely to prayer.

The successors of Brochwel confirmed that Pennant should be 'a perpetual sanctuary, asylum, and a safe refuge for the wretched'. The hares in the neighbourhood became known as 'ŵyn Melangell' (Monacella's lambs). Local inhabitants would not dare kill a hare especially if it was on Sanctuary land, and if any one called 'God and St Melangell preserve thee' when a hare was being chased, it would escape.

At the east end of the church is a small chamber called 'Cell y Bedd' (cell of the grave). And written in the old parish register of 1680, are the following lines:

'Mil engyl a Melangell
Trechant lu fyddin y fall.'

(Melangell with a thousand angels, shall triumph over the whole power of hell.)

Like with most legends, there are variations to it, e.g. some state that Monacella was the daughter of King Iochwel of Ireland and others that she was the daughter of Tudwal ap Ceredic. Nevertheless, some unknown carver of the fifteenth century has preserved for us the legend in the chancel screen of Pennant Melangell.

When Parker was installing the marigold window in the west wall of Llanyblodwel church in 1856, his workmen discovered three fragments of inscribed stone embedded in the rough masonry. They bear the design of a hare being chased by a greyhound, similar to that on the screen at Pennant Melangell. These fragments were subsequently inserted into the wall of the south porch. The hare is also to be found carved on the chancel screen within the church.

(iv) St Anno, Llananno, Radnorshire.

Radnorshire, as well as Montgomeryshire, had its attractions for John Parker, and nowhere more so than the little church of Llananno by the river Ithon. His first of many visits was on 18th September, 1828, and inside 'the docile and unsightly barn, for the church at Llananno has no pretensions of any sort of architectural beauty', he found that the:

'chancel screen is not in quite such a state of preservation as I expected. Here as in all the others, one part of the woodwork having severed, the whole fabric has been slightly distorted and several of the exposed ornaments are thrown out of their places. Almost half the panelled ceiling on the south side is gone. The greater part of the crockets belonging to the canopies were also missing and their adjoining pinnacles. One whole border is lost and another small one is only guessed at by a small fragment. Yet, the parts which remain are so rich and the original effect may be so clearly perceived that I have never been more gratified than with the western side of this chancel screen. It seems to have been the object of the architect here, as at Llanwnog, to produce, if I may so express myself, an effervescence of richness. The whole work has a delicate frothy lightness which when it was entire must have had a most elegant effect. In the tracery between the mullions there is more variety than high wrought workmanship. The central arch however, is a most exquisite instance of curvilinear tracery. The running fretwork pattern over this harmonizes perfectly with all the rest of the screen . . . By examining all the old nooks and cornices and heaps of rubbish thrown about, I succeeded in restoring some original patterns of panelling which were all broken to pieces, altho' they merited a better fate. I even sent a boy to Llanbister to buy some nails that might unite these precious fragments once more, but the wood became so unsound from damp and age that all my endeavours to make a permanent restoration were ineffectual. The nails had no hold upon the crumbling wood and I gave up my attempt after making a careful drawing.'

In the Autumn of 1829 he made another visit, and this time he noted that of the thirty two panels that had once been on the ceiling of the chancel screen, only twenty two remained. Two others he found in fragments which he carefully put together so as to determine the original pattern. The remainder were lost!

He made at least fourteen drawings of this screen and if it had suffered the fate of so many screens in the nineteenth century we have at least his drawings showing its splendour and beauty. With the destruction of the screen at Newtown, the one at Llananno must still rank as one of the best known and most ornate example of its kind in Wales.

His closing remarks after one visit was that his researches at Llananno had been very satisfactory, and that several curious and elegant relics of Gothic art had been rescued from oblivion during his two days' examination of the rood loft. 'Llananno is perfectly unknown to the architectural tourist,' he wrote. He wanted several days more to study the running borders as they deserved more attention than he had been able to give them. They could only be 'understood or copied by long and continued attention and repeated surveys', and this was his personal philosophy in all that he did, and particularly so with regard to anything at all to do with his passion for Gothic art.

If the chancel screen at Llananno, placed as it is in a small rustic church, is indicative of the screens which have been destroyed by time and neglect, then our loss has indeed been great.

His Journals contain many more references to chancel screens and fonts in rural churches and although they may not all merit much attention by the general public, they were important to Parker and his meticulous drawings and detailed descriptions have ensured that their future is safeguarded. The loving care which their original craftsmen displayed has been repeated in his Journals and drawings.

(v) The Abbey of Cwm Hir, Radnorshire.

On the 5th February, 1828, Parker left on a pilgrimage to the Abbey of Cwm Hir in Radnorshire. The weather was very fine for the time of year and the landscape afforded him endless variety of colouring. He passed through Llanbadarn Fynydd where the church looked 'like a wretched barn outside, but contained the remnants of a chancel screen once highly wrought in Gothic patterns'. He failed to gain access to Llananno church but vowed to return.

He stopped at Llanddewi Ystradenni where he obtained accommodation for the night since he was only four miles from his destination – the Abbey of Cwm Hir.

This Cistercian Abbey was founded in the year 1143 by Maredudd, Cadwallon and Einion, sons of Madoc, Lord of Maelienydd.

In 1401-1402, Owain Glyndŵr sent out predatory expeditions against the English settlers in Wales and against such Welshmen who refused to aid his cause. Montgomeryshire suffered much from these expeditions. The Abbey of Cwm Hir was also destroyed. Some restoration work was carried out and in 1539 the Abbey was finally dissolved by Henry VIII.

It is known that in 1542 some of the beautiful arcades and clustered columns of the Abbey were broken down and carried away to be used in the restoration of Llanidloes church.

The site of the Abbey was excavated in 1837 but unfortunately no plans or record of the excavations were preserved.

In about 1824 a Mr Thomas Wilson purchased the Abbey and he caused the site of the church to be cleared of the rubbish with which it was covered.

Since Parker visited the site in February, 1828 his copious notes are all the more important and warrant inclusion in full:

'On Wednesday, February 6th, I left Llanddewi about nine o'clock and went on foot in quest of this far-famed Abbey. After walking for about 4 miles and a half through dirty lanes, I found myself within a field of my destination. The whole scenery has so great a resemblance to that of the Abbey of Valle Crucis near Llangollen that any one who has been there may easily conceive the situation of Abbey Cwm Hir. For it is not more romantic, perhaps the two sites are about equal. But Cwm Hir altho' in days of yore, much more noted than Valle Crucis Abbey, and in its influence upon Gothic art, much more active, has now become a total ruin barely picturesque and utterly devoid of grandeur. The footpath led me by the side of what seemed more like a large court than the interior of a church, and I remarked a great regularity throughout the design. First of all I examined an old chapel where service continues to be performed but contains nothing worth notice. It stands two or three hundred yards above the ruins and between them are several houses, buildings and trees. The farm nearest the ruins is occupied I believe by Mr Thomas who holds the living of Llananno and Llanbadarn Fynydd. I then procured a yard for I had come without my measuring tape, and on going to the ruins was told that a Mr Wilson, the proprietor, had a dispute about tithes or something of that kind and had forbidden the measurement of any land about the Abbey. However, I soon made it clear that I had come there merely to examine ruins and went on without clearly comprehending the cause of his prohibition. On measuring the walls and columns I found that much might be proved from the scanty relics that remain. It appears that the conventual church of Cwm Hir was designed on a scale of unusual grandeur. The nave and an aisle only seem to have been completed but the eastern part of it was of course used as a choir. This part of the church is two hundred and fifty feet long and seventy two broad, inside measurements. The nave is 40 feet wide from the centre of each column and the whole is one regular oblong. Twenty six clustered columns each 4ft 5in in diameter and in two rows divide the side aisle from the nave and thirty four pilasters of corresponding style are still almost remaining on the walls. An unusual fate seems to have befallen this Abbey of loosing all remains of its windows and arches. There is a small waste collection of varied fragments carefully preserved and piled upon each other at the chancel end of the church but the windows and arches are not to be discovered. The different capitals of the clustered columns are so numerous that many details can be proved from them. This church seems to have been extremely regular. The nave rose considerably higher than the side aisle as appears by one stone among the fragments, where at the side of a foliaged capital is a shaft, which established the fact of a clerestory. This is confirmed by capitals among fragments larger than the others, the only appropriate place for which would have been at a higher elevation. The clustered columns or pilasters on the side walls are of three slender shafts, those at the corners were of two. What the roof may have been we can hardly conjecture but as all trace of this has vanished it is likely that it was of wood especially that of the nave where the space is unusually wide compared with the side aisles. Some small fragments of mullions belonging to the windows are to be met with, but they prove nothing except that the windows were not of the English Gothic. The side aisle must have been very lofty for no trace of windows appear altho' the walls in some places are as high as thirteen or fourteen feet but a sort of bank probably created by the fall of the upper walls gives the whole interior an appearance of being excavated, and much lower than the surrounding level.

I looked in vain for marks in the ground or wall that might point out the situation of the gorgeous chancel screen which has been so fortunately preserved by its removal to the church at Newtown. If the roof of this Abbey church were in a style of equal splendour the effect of the interior from either end must have been unrivalled and that such a display of Gothic art could be found in so complete solitude must ever cause wonder for the remaining fragments are richly carved in a very fine stone which must have been brought from some distance altho' for the body of the walls the slaty stone of the neighbourhood is employed. Though the present ruins are too destitute of architectural forms to produce a grand effect, yet if the fragments that remain were put into their proper places, respecting which a Gothic architect would have no doubt, this ruin, without any fanciful additions, might become a beautiful and imposing object. The dimensions are already magnificent and a very trifling aid from cement and mortar would elicit in some degree those latent glories which are lost to all but antiquarian observers. The situation of the Abbey is by no means the dreary spot that I supposed, the surrounding hills do not exclude the winter sun and in February, when it might have appeared forbidding, the temperature of the air was delightfully mild. The climate of this valley must assuredly be temperate for no violent wind can sweep over it from any quarter – it is completely sheltered. The principal mountain in sight lies to the westward and is called Camlo. The Clywedog, a small stream, flows within a field on the south side of the ruins. On the north a steep sloping hill said to be 1511 feet high is called the Great Park, where in former days this establishment kept three hundred head of deer. Birch Hill about 1751 feet high rises to the south and presents a picturesque scene of scattered wood of birch trees.

When I consider the dimensions of this once magnificent Abbey as compared with those of our Cathedrals all of which they rival or exceed, I am struck with astonishment that such immense pile, and of such costly workmanship, should have been erected in a spot which is remote from all the influence created by similar works of art. In the heart of Radnorshire, the wildest of all Welsh counties, in a neighbourhood where the roads must always have been difficult for travellers, in this lonely though beautiful retreat, arose one of the purest and richest models of sacred architecture that could be found in the kingdom.'

Chapter 11

Nonconformity

Although the period 1750-1850 is regarded as the golden age of the travellers it was also a period when radical changes were taking part in all walks of life in Wales. But it is surprising that so few travellers took any notice of them.

Many of the early travellers have made references to the churches of Wales and this is only to be expected since so many of them were clergymen. Their interest, however, was purely superficial and their writings are generally confined to the fabric of the buildings.

These were the days of Howell Harris and the advancement of nonconformity. The 1840's also experienced the activities of Rebecca and her Daughters particularly in South Wales, who were protesting vigorously against the payment of tolls on the public highways. Very few of the travellers made any reference to them. J.H. Cliffe in his *Notes and Recollections of an Angler* refers to an encounter which he had with them once in 1843 in the following words:

> 'We found ourselves in the immediate presence of the dreaded "Rebecca". Within less than twenty paces, at least twenty tall dark-looking figures lay basking in the moonlight on the roadside, prepared, as we supposed, to dispute the road with every passer-by. We had come upon these men so silently, that we must have taken them by surprise as we rushed past them with headlong speed. We were tolerably agile then, and being in good training, we managed to get over the ground with marvellous celerity.'

Parker was also in South Wales in September, 1843 and whilst he did not encounter them, he noted in his Journal that 'there is much less travelling than usual through South Wales this year, chiefly due to the riots of Rebecca and her Daughters. These disturbances of the peace are doing mischief in Carmarthenshire and the adjoining County.

Nonconformity was also of interest to the travellers but almost always in a derogatory fashion. One traveller who took a great interest in the churches was Sir Thomas Gery Cullum, himself a clergyman, but the prevalence of Methodism was a great annoyance to him, so much so that he made a special visit to Talgarth, Breconshire, to see for himself what was going on there. His remarks, although prejudiced, are very interesting:

'Lady Huntingdon's fanatic Madness has here (at Brecon) likewise exemplified itself in a small neat Chapel, where I heard a shabby Fellow with a coloured Handkerchief about his Neck, in an unanimated but noisy Harrangue to a full Audience, drowning the sound of the neighbouring stream. It was in Welsh, so I could not understand it.

But it is at Talgarth that her Enthusiasm displays itself in its utmost Extravagance. She has there instituted what she calls a College, which is a Seminary for young Men to be brought up in her own Tenets, and sent into the world to propagate them. I had the curiosity to visit this extraordinary Foundation . . . This Sect are certainly now very bad Members of Society, and may become most dangerous Instruments in the hand of some future Cromwell. Near this Seminary is the neat house where Howell Harris lived, a famous fanatic.'

Another aspect of Methodism which amused the travellers was the sect generally referred to as the 'Jumpers'. William Hutton from Birmingham was a regular visitor to North Wales, and in 1803 he published his 'Remarks Upon North Wales' being the result of sixteen tours. In September, 1799 he was at Caernarfon and had already attended two services at the Parish church of Llanbeblig where he found the congregation to number just sixteen. He then heard that the 'Jumpers' were to hold a meeting in the town and he decided to join the congregation out of curiosity. The chapel was crowded and he had to jostle his way in.

As the service proceeded, the crowd 'broke out into the most rapturous violence of voice and gesture', and so the uproar continued until 'One hundred different tunes, yelling from one hundred different voices in a single room produced horror in the extreme. I never experienced sound more discordant'. The congregation then started to jump and as soon as one started another joined him until the whole congregation was jumping and the 'person who was the happiest was he who would exert the loudest, continue the longest, and jump the highest'.

Not all travellers enjoyed their sojourn in Wales, and Sir Robert Kerr

Porter was one of those. During his tour in 1799 he had very few kind things to write about. When he arrived at Capel Curig he was soon surrounded by a mob of drunken Welshmen who were 'all bloody, dirty, and scratches which they had obtained singing Psalms and fighting'. The bedroom at the Inn where he stayed was festooned with cobwebs and had only a chair and stool for furniture and dirty woollen petticoats and old stockings were hanging on the walls.

His feelings about the Welsh and their religion were no better, and although he had only been in the area for a short period of time, he felt confident enough to express his opinions as to their character when he wrote:

'The Welsh are extremely selfish, and if it is at all possible to cheat and in any way to take in a stranger they will. If one settles amongst them as farmer or otherwise, every way is used to injure him, they hamstring his cattle, open his gates and break his enclosures, in short everything possible by which they can annoy him they do, but in some degree, this may be accounted for, they are uncommonly Methodists and consequently Devils. The women are of a most disagreeable disposition, one moment all good humour and affability, the next all sulking and apparently without any cause whatsoever. They are continually knitting, both walking and sitting in their Religious Bawling Houses.'

Porter travelled widely in Europe and in Russia where he was ultimately appointed court painter to the Tsar. He eventually married a Princess of the Russian Court. He possessed the aptitude of ingratiating himself with people of every rank particularly in the Courts of Europe where he received many honours.

Although many travellers make references to the Methodists, detailed accounts of their services are not frequently met with in their reports and are therefore all the more interesting.

Parker likewise took a keen interest in the religious life of Wales, and the frequency of his visits gave him a much better opportunity to acquaint himself of the situation. His Journals abound with references to services which he attended although he had no knowledge of the Welsh language. He was well known in Llanberis and Capel Curig in particular, so much so, that he was asked to take the service at Capel Curig on one occasion:

'Sunday, July 1st. At breakfast this morning the waiter came and told me that Mr Hughes was very ill and that a Dr Taylor, a clergyman from Essex, had offered to read English prayers, but could not give the congregation a sermon as he had a cold, and he asked if I could preach in Welsh, I said that I could not, but that if the congregation could understand me I should have no objection to preach in English and sent my compliments to Dr Taylor to this effect. As, however, it was now church time it seemed rather too late for any such arrangement, and I was walking down to the church with Mr Dugmore, a gentleman from Norfolk, with whom I had met by accident, when the waiter came up with Dr Taylor's compliments to say that he should be very glad if I could take the sermon. I then went back to the Inn, put on bands and took a sermon out of my carpet bag with which I went down to the church. The service had just begun when I entered. There was good singing and about half the congregation understood English. After the Communion service I put on the surplice as there was no black gown and preached. The congregation appeared attentive. Dr Taylor and Mr Dugmore, after I had ended, expressed their approbation of my sermon.'

He also regularly attended the church at Nant Peris, but on one occasion in 1832, he was most dissatisfied with the service which was being conducted by the Rector, the Revd Henry Bayley Williams, the son of the Revd Peter Bayley Williams, Rector of Llanrug with whom Parker was acquainted. The reason for his disapproval was that the Rector had placed his hat and cloak on the Communion Table during the service, as indeed had a number of the congregation. Parker was most punctilious that the church services should always be held with great reverence and strictly in accordance with the approved services of the Church of England. His Journals contain many references to this particular point when he expressed his dissatisfaction with any service that was conducted without due reverence.

After the service was over, he passed a little cottage where a dissenting minister of the Independent Persuasion was addressing a crowded congregation. He was a middle aged man, rather good looking and a schoolmaster whose residence was a few miles away. He was in good voice, but with a drawl at the end of his words or sentence and he used 'much action, sometimes one, sometimes both hands, not however affectedly, but only when it seemed natural to him'.

Eye witness accounts of services in the early Methodists chapels are few and far between because the travellers had no real interest in them. Whilst we do have contemporary accounts in various histories of the Methodist Movement in Welsh they do tend to give a one-sided impression. Parker, on the other hand, as one of the few travellers who was intrigued by all that was going on around him, has given a very detailed account of a service which he attended at Llanberis in 1832, and as such accounts are so infrequently met with, I think that it is important enough to be quoted in full:

'I returned to the Inn with my guide and after dinner strolled out above the dissenting chapel or the Welsh Calvinistic Methodists a few hundred yards from the Inn. The weather was beautifully fine and when I saw the congregation collecting I went into the Chapel myself. The building filled up by slow degrees, first the ground floor, and then the two galleries at each end of it for it was joined at one end to a house and had no windows but at the sides, one being the pulpit. It was a long time before any minister appeared and one psalm after another was sung by a set of regular singers, only a few of the congregation joining them. At length two ministers made an appearance, in dress and outward look not at all superior to some of the neighbouring farmers. One of them begun by reading a Chapter of Scripture, then followed an extempore prayer without much gesture and with eyes closed in the manner of the Scottish Kirk. Then there was a Psalm well sung with the congregation joining in; rather too loud and solemn but impressive. The other minister now came forward and read a Chapter and then gave out the text in Welsh, after which he translated it into English and expounded in that language, making excuses for his awkwardness not having expected, he said, to find it necessary to do so until he had come to the pulpit. This I believe was in consequence of his having caught my eye soon after he had arrived and saw that I was a stranger and an Englishman. In his exposition of the text "Know therefore, brethren that by this man is preached unto you the forgiveness of sin', there was no false doctrine but a slowness and dryness of expression and manner that strongly contrasted with what followed. He soon began to address the congregation in Welsh and for some time he and they were temperate in their behaviour. But by degrees the tone of his voice became wilder, and I should observe that both these men and the other at Llanberis, had a most singular mode of quavering upon syllables at the end or middle of sentences, and prolonging the vowels to almost any extent, by doing so they could bring every sentence however worded into the same rhythm. This extraordinary licence, had however become too familiar both to them and the congregation that the sense did not seem to be utterly destroyed by it altho' of course it was much obscured. When this had gone on for some time, it became as it were contagious and the congregation responded in the same tones. The preacher now became still more violent, he stamped his feet, flung his arms and raved! Then some women began to cry in reply and at last his voice was drowned in their outcries. He continued for a wonderful length of time roaring and raving while they rivalled him, as being several against one. At last he ended, a psalm was then sung very loud. Whenever it was not loud the confused cries of the women broke upon my ear, then again drowned in the swell of the psalmody. The congregation were now leaving the chapel and I observed two women who were in a sort of convulsion near the pulpit. These had been most violent in their ejaculations. Returning to the Inn after the service, which had lasted from seven to nine, I was told by the mistress of the Inn that they heard loud crying still going on at the chapel. It was now 10 o'clock, I went there again and witnessed a scene of horror that I shall never forget. There were four boys and about 6 girls, the girls about 15 or 16 years old, the boys younger, all raving mad! Their friends looking on while these unhappy wretches unconscious of all around them, did nothing but ejaculate without intermission, lifting their arms and rolling over the pews and benches. Two candles lighted in a wooden chandelier threw a faint light over the melancholy scene. The preachers of course were not there but the effect of their frantic raving remained long after them. They slept however in the adjoining building. Some of the boys were led away about eleven o'clock raving and shouting along the road. Such was the conclusion of the dissenting worship in this chapel. I cannot believe after what I had witnessed, that these ministers preached the wording of truth and soberness. I heard the same cries from my bedroom window at nearly twelve o'clock. These horrid scenes are of course the predisposing cause of mental and bodily diseases to a great extent and accordingly the neighbourhood is full of anecdotes relating to the sickness and death of those concerned in them. The state of the congregation in the chapel when the preacher concluded bore a strong resemblance to the excitement produced by a popish miracle, and I cannot help comparing it with a well known specimen of Romish fraud – the liquefaction of the blood of St Januarius.

The madness and superstition exhibit the same features in almost all ages, countries and nations. The dissenting preachers have now so thoroughly roused the passion of their hearers for excitement that everything else is cast away to admit that feeling. Hence they sacrifice without remorse the minds, and indeed the bodies of their younger auditors, and labour to procure the various degrees of anxiety, till they succeed at length in causing perfect frenzy. This is their triumph, and it is one characteristic of the vulgar, that they think no end is gained, no power of truth shown, unless reason herself is overwhelmed in the conflict. Yet, the harangues which cause all this excitement are not, I believe, at all distinguished for scope of language or highly varied thought, they abound in repetitions, and in this I blame the preacher, not having it in his power to control himself and them; he does not reign his feelings, but aims at something superhuman.

The preachers I heard at Llanberis appear to be opium eaters. It is very painful to see a large number of people under so strong a delusion that they still continue to frequent these meetings where any man of sober mind must feel that insanity has been taught as an art and practised as a virtue.

But I cannot help hoping and believing that public opinion will at length turn against these caricatures of devotion and that our primitive church will regain her influence when these errors have passed away. Can such men as these overthrow an apostolic establishment?'

Once again we see the importance which he placed on the sedate and steady character of the Church of England services and the reverence which he thought was so essential in any form of worship. Although the language was strange to him he had been able to gauge the feelings expressed at that particular service.

He remained at Llanberis for just a few days after that service during which time he made a sketch of Dolbadarn Castle and visited Tŷ Du which had once been the residence of Bishop Goodman when he had to flee from prosecution.

Chapter 12

The Journal – September, 1831

The year 1831 was a particularly busy one for Parker insofar as travelling was concerned because he made at least four separate visits to Wales during that year. In September, he made an interesting tour through mid-Wales and his journal of that particular tour makes very absorbing reading because it is possible for us to re-live the difficulties of cross-country travelling during the time when roads were almost non-existent and to savour the pleasure of dancing the quadrille to the music of the flute at Llandrindod Wells. It is also interesting for the variety of experiences which he describes, and he ends the journal as he so often did, with an appreciation of those experiences, difficult though they may have been at times.

'On Tuesday September 20th, 1831, I left Pennarth in a gig with my man servant about 10 o'clock and went through Newtown to Llanidloes, which is 13 miles from Newtown and more than 15 from Pennarth. Whenever I pass Caersws I admire the situation and wonder that the chief town of the neighbourhood should ever have occupied the situation of Newtown. I called at Pen y Bont on Mr O. Crewe who was not at home. His house commands a most elegant view of the Severn in the neighbourhood of Llandinam, and the church if it were at all picturesque would form a beautiful central object in the landscape. Passing Llandinam I called at Berth Ddu on Mr Brown who was not at home. Further on I made a small vignette of some wooded hills above the Severn. Met the coach coming from Llanidloes. Weather cold and signs of rain. At Llanidloes I had luncheon at the Inn and went to the church where I examined the fine old font, now quite neglected, and lying under the belfry in a heap of rubbish. Three men moved it into a situation where I drew it. The stem was in a separate stone and I contrived at length to ascertain what this font was, and made measurements and a drawing of it. In an hour and a half I left Llanidloes in rain which continued until I reached Llangurig. Here it ceased for a while and I spent 25 minutes in the church examining and measuring the chancel screen of which I have already made a drawing. It is very much mutilated. The carving is not so delicate as it seemed to me two years ago. It is of late but nevertheless pure Gothic. The font I also measured. The crockets of the tracery in the screen are but coarsely done. On leaving this lonely village, I traversed a long extent of dreary moorland vales, with a few scattered habitations, and the infant Wye meandering through rushy meadows until we arrived at Eisteddfa Gerrig within 2 miles of the summit of Plynlimon. Here a new Inn has been built and two bedrooms may be had, they talk of enlarging it greatly next summer. This is the highest level of the road between Newtown and Aberystwyth. Nothing can exceed the loneliness of the surrounding scenery, but it is entirely destitute of grandeur. At this place I had a glass of whisky and water, a very needful resource, for the wind and rain has become almost incessant. On leaving this place the road gradually descended and, on the edge of night after passing a long tract of newly made road, I found myself at a new Inn near Pont Yrrwyd, and an overhanging cascade that falls into the Rheidiol. This picturesque object in some degree, consoled me for having lost my way, which however, I soon regained and after a drive of two miles and a half I arrived at the Devil's Bridge, while the gloom of night threw a romantic mysteriousness over the grandeur of the scenery. I dined or rather supped at about 8 o'clock at the Hafod Arms. Next morning, I was called at seven and on entering the sitting room I saw a view out of the window, a view combining all that a painter can desire in such a subject – romantic rocky banks adorned with timber and copsewood – a cascade in the centre and the stony channel of the Rheidiol beneath – while the distance was composed of cloudless heathy mountain scenery. The morning sun threw fine shadows over all the banks of the river, and I hardly ever beheld a scene so thoroughly harmonious in outline and colouring. Of this I made a sketch before and after breakfast, then I went down below the bridge and made another of the chasm and the two bridges above it. This was a difficult subject to arrange properly, but the colouring and form of the rocks are splendid. There is more evidence of river-agency here than usual, even the upper rocks are water-worn. After this I went down in front of the Inn – there is a path which is tolerably safe to a certain point, below which it becomes truly dangerous, I wonder that something is not done to make this pathway more easy. At present the steps are all leaning towards the precipice and the steepness was alarming to me tho' accustomed always to a romantic footpath. From hence I intended crossing the river to get on the opposite bank which must I suppose command a fine view but the river was too full and there is no bridge.

I returned to the Hafod Arms, bill reasonable, settled it, and went off in a gig to Hafod. A rude pointed arch upon high ground among larch plantations formed the first indication of our approach to the grounds, and on descending through trees for above a mile and a half we entered the lodge where nothing remarkable appears. After a long sylvan drive, the Ystwyth on the left and beyond it a woody mountain we reached a spacious lawn sloping to the south surrounded by fine oak and in the midst of which appeared a mansion of extremely bad modern Gothic yet palace like in its general effect and in the happiest of all situation. If this building were in pure taste Hafod would surely be one of the wonders of the world. The whole aspect of the place bespeaks of it being the residence of a gentleman and a scholar, the splendid retirement of wealth and learning. Hafod is quite a phenomenon among mansions, worthy of a better fate than it had hitherto met with or is likely to meet, for this place having once been destroyed by fire and now just from chancery, will they say, be pulled down entirely unless it is purchased with all the surrounding property which however is not large. Mrs Johns, the relic of Mr Johns the founder is yet alive and resides in Devonshire. Mr Smith, a banker in London was executor to Mr Johns and he has lately died and his partner Mr Harrison is now the manager of the property. He comes here twice a year to receive rent, stays about a week each time and then Hafod resumes its usual solitude except when visited by strangers.

The house is built of a warm grey coloured stone and is composed of a square central mass with pavilions or nearly detached rooms at the corners. Externally, the intended effect is Gothic but miserably modern. Inside the decorations are entirely Grecian. This I always consider as a kind of architectural hypocrisy, much to be condemned, fashionable a few years ago, but now I hope, discarded for ever. There cannot be a greater mistake than to suppose that Gothic does not suit interiors, on the contrary, the chief advantage of the style is in all internal arrangements, in vaulted ceilings and doorways.

The furniture at Hafod is magnificent. There are slabs of green granite and tables of oriental alabaster – columns and entablature of verd antique – chimney pieces of statuary marble exquisitely wrought, enclosing bass reliefs of Greek sculpture. Some of the most precious books were preserved from the fire but in one room alone, volumes to the amount of £20,000 value were destroyed. An elegant small group by Banks of 'Thetis plunging Achilles in the Stynx' is placed in the room called the long library. There is a restored Greek Bacchus larger than life in the central hall. Some chairs corresponding with Goblin tapestry burnt at the fire still remain. A curious old Greek painting once belonging to a Monastery in Carmarthenshire, presented to an ancestor of Mr Johns is preserved in one of the libraries, of which there are no less than three in this abode of literature and study. It is in the style of Giotto and Cimabue and the subject is 'Elijah'. Other rooms contain a very fine Salvator – 'The Ruined Alchymist', an appropriate subject for that painter, a fine Van Dyke 'The Descent from the Cross', a very gloomy coloured picture. A 'Holy Family' by Rubens in beautiful preservation, an elaborate 'Assumption of the Virgin' by Benedetto Lutti, and a fine 'Ecce Homo' by Muralez, a Spanish painter surnamed el Divino. The first room contains a large Rubens the subject 'Decius devoting himself'. One of the libraries contains very fine illuminated manuscripts in vellum. For one of these works Napoleon is said to have offered an immense price without success. On the upper part of the walls are subjects by Stoddart in the style of the classical processions but the costume and story selected from Froissart and other chroniclers, they are paintings in imitation of basso relievo. The house at Hafod is already surpassed by many built since the period of its erection, but the exquisite situation is perhaps unrivalled. A bust of Mr Johns is placed in the entrance, the features are remarkably like those of George IVth.

Hafod is 14 miles from Aberystwyth the nearest market, a serious objection, which no fortune however large, could altogether overcome. In the woods above the house a small church appears built at the same time as the mansion. The top of its very small spire is however, the only part that is in view. Leaving the house, which four other visitors had seen with me, I drove the gig to the beginning of a path from which I was guided by a boy to the flower garden much neglected and overgrown and rather damp from too much foliage. Following the course of the Ystwyth I arrived at two small falls over which two bridges are built like those of the Devil's Bridge, the old arch becoming ruinous, a new higher one was raised upon its piers. Here I made a sketch, it was a small but rather picturesque subject. Here Edmund met me with the gig and I then drove on through oak woods to a more open valley, where supposing that I saw the Inn of Cwm Ystwyth at a distance, I sent him to order dinner while I began

Sweeney Hall, near Oswestry

John Parker's Grave at Llanyblodwel

Photo: Edgar W. Parry

St Llwchaiarn Church, Llanmerewig

John Parker, 1836 (National Library of Wales)

Parker's pulpit-cum-reading desk at St Llwchaiarn

Frontispiece of John Parker's Book 'The Passengers'
Published in 1831.

John Parker (National Library of Wales)

Llyn y Dywarchen, Caernarfonshire

*The ruins of the Abbey of Cwm Hir looking eastwards
up the nave of the Abbey church, 1895.*

A page from 'The Upland Parish' (Llanmerewig) by John Parker.
Illustrated by his sister Lady Mary Leighton
(by kind permission of Sir Michael Leighton Bart).

Interior of Llanyblodwel Church showing part of screen and Reredos.

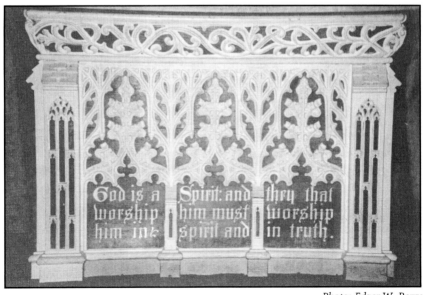

God is a Spirit: and they that worship him must worship him in spirit and in truth.

The Altar Table designed by John Parker

John Parker 1856 (National Library of Wales)

The Habitat of the Wood-sorrel (Oxalis acetosella)
(See detailed notes on pages 42-43)

Chancel screen, Newtown (Detail).

Eastern view of chancel screen, Llanwnog.

John Parker, 1837 (National Library of Wales)

Legand of St Monacella on screen at Pennant Melangell

John Parker, 1828 (National Library of Wales)

Chancel screen, Llananno.

Hafod (by H. Gastineau, c. 1830)

The 'Wonder', London and Shrewsbury Coach.
John Parker travelled on the 'Wonder' Coach from Oswestry to
Snowdonia on many occasions.

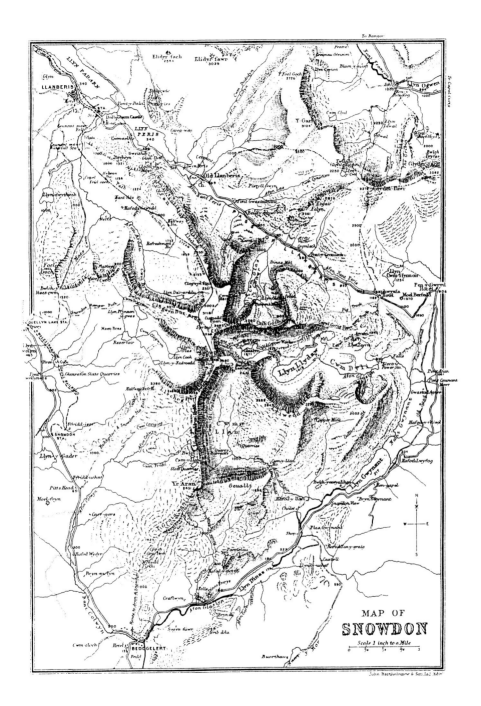

MAP OF
SNOWDON
Scale 1 inch to a Mile

John Bartholomew & Son Ltd. Edin

Valle Crucis Abbey, Llangollen.
(by kind permission of Mrs Lavinia Bonnor-Maurice).

Pontcysyllte Aqueduct and the vale of Llangollen
(by kind permission of Mrs Lavinia Bonnor-Maurice).

John Parker (National Library of Wales)

The Nave, St David's Cathedral, 1836

93

John Parker (National Library of Wales)

*A page from his Gothic Poem, 'Snowdonia',
illustrated by his sister Lady Mary Leighton.*

John Parker, 1828 (National Library of Wales)

Chancel screen, Clynnog Fawr

John Parker

Bala Lake
(by kind permission of Mrs Lavinia Bonnor-Maurice).

John Parker, 1848 (National Library of Wales)

Poppy heads and chancel screen at Conwy Church

a retrospective sketch of Hafod. Before I had done much Edmund returned with the gig saying that the house, altho' once an Inn, was now a private residence. After finishing my sketch I drove on to the lead mines of Cwm Ystwyth, in a dreary glen, thence through Cwm Ystwyth to the Lisburne Arms, a small Inn where I got some chops, and bread and cheese. This place is 7 miles from the Devil's Bridge. On leaving it, the road leads over a rather handsome bridge of one arch ornamented with some carving on the centre, and then goes up a dreary hill after which the road becomes worse and the landscape more desolate than the neighbourhood of Steddfa Gerrig. After traversing a long extent of moorland vale where human habitations were not seen for miles together, and crossing one extremity of Montgomeryshire, we followed the dreary banks of the River Elan for some time and then began to ascend the longest and loftiest hill that I ever went up in any country by a regular road, excepting Mont Cenis and Simplon. Two miles and a half of constant ascent brought us to the summit of a mountain range and Cob was almost knocked up with fatigue, tho' Edmund and I walked the whole way. This immense hill is called Pen Rhiw Wen – The White Steep Hill – no tree, no house, no shelter appears anywhere, not even rock, but boggy moors, immeasurably spread like those of Scotland or the dreary west of Ireland. What a change from the delicious woodland luxuriance of Hafod. In the desolate highland vale where the Elan flows, I remarked a small farm house without a tree near it, but sheltered from the south west by a steep green bank parallel to the river and rising twice as high as the building.

From the Devil's Bridge to Rhayadr is considered about 20 miles. On reaching the highest level, the moon rose, and was a great service in showing a rather romantic defile down which a road without either wall or hedge descended rapidly. At the bottom of this ravine which I believe is called Cwm Gamallt, there is a very small water called Llyn Gwynllan formerly a much larger one if the appearance of the meadows near it may be a fair criterion, for they are quite flat and from them the mountain rises abruptly. There are some fine rocks here and some groves of oak trees. Descending into Rhayadr we passed Mr Piggot's of Drew close to the town, then crossed the bridge and stopped at the Red Lion. In the sitting room I met Mr Sace, an engineer and a Mr Merryweather, I believe a Clergyman married to a Radnorshire lady. He had succeeded in taking a salmon, a 9 pounder, that day, but not in good condition.

Thursday, September 22nd. After breakfast about nine o'clock I went out to the bridge from which there are some tolerably picturesque views. The Wye here is rocky. The bridge is one of one wide arch. Above the town is the church, a small building utterly devoid of interest, and on the opposite side of the river is another called Cwm Teithyr, Welsh and English duty is performed alternately in these churches. Leaving Rhayadr, the road ascended and the retrospect is not unpleasing. The glen of the Elan at some distance with the moorland mountains formed a background for the town of Rhayadr which however, has no conspicuous church tower, a peculiar feature, to recommend it. Cwm Elan belongs to a Mr Peel. At a few miles distance I passed Llwyn Barryat, a mansion lately belonging to a Mr Evans, whose property lying about the neighbourhood is about 2000 a year. The present heir is a minor. The well wooded grounds of this house with a wide horizon of lofty moor and partial cultivation, formed a subject which I adopted for my sketch book. Further on I came to the brow of a hill which commanded Llanbadarn Fawr with a richly wooded extent of hill and valley bounded by the high moors of Radnor Forest and finely coloured. Here a pelting storm came on. At a turnpike about 8½ miles from Rhayadr I turned at right angles with the road leading to Llandrindod Wells about 4 miles off. Llandrindod is therefore about 12 miles from Rhayadr. I passed the church of Llanbadarn Fawr where I expected some fine Gothic as it was a monastic foundation. But nothing now remains except a barbaric Norman door within the south porch where some animals with curling fleur de lys tails are rudely carved, with a head placed between them like an escutcheon. The door within the arch is flat headed. Some very small windows of early Gothic light the east and south side of this church. Here I thought I should have met with a Gothic rood loft but was disappointed as on looking through the windows no such thing appeared, all was modern. On reaching Llandrindod Common I was in doubt whether to turn up to the Pump House which appeared in a sheltered situation on the left as I had always heard of the Inn here as being in a most exposed and barren situation. On reaching it, I found a small house in reality larger than it appears, fronting to the south-west, the outside walls boarded – a common practice in this country, and altho' a windy spot not so barren or cheerless as I supposed. At the back of the Inn are some woody arches, in front is the Saline Pump over which a small room and porch are built with an adjoining walk sheltered by some fir trees and hedge. At the side of the approach among alder trees, the sulphur spring rises within a pump and trough but not honoured with any building or enclosure. At the Inn I understood they can make up more than one hundred beds but they have only two parlours, both of course public, one for dining and the other occupied at all other times by the parties in the house. Thus a travelling family coming to Llandrindod, after the public dinner was over, and perhaps fatigued and sleepy after a long journey, would be ushered at once into the public sitting room where they would in general find a dress party, sitting around the fire after dinner. This room, or bedroom, would be then their only choice. I found only two or three persons in the public room, but the rest being absent on an excursion for the day. A Clergyman whose name is Thoresby of Cusop or some such place in Herefordshire walked with me for some time before dinner. I took a glass of the sulphurous water.

The views about Llandrindod are extensive and picturesque with a pleasing mixture of loneliness and woody cultivation. Several well composed landscapes might be obtained from the neighbourhood but without much rock. The lower grounds are much diversified with scattered woods and heathy commons or green pasture bordering the River Ithon. In general, the arrangement of the scenery here is neither rich nor bold but is what an artist would call 'masterly'. Partaking of a two-fold character of the vale and the plain it exhibits all the fine characters of aerial perspective. Mr Morris Lloyd of Montgomery and Mrs Pugh of Llannerch y Ddôl with a large party arrived from an excursion before dinner and at about half past four we sat down 24 to dinner. Mr Lloyd had succeeded in catching about 15 samlets and one 4 pound salmon. The most usual hour for the table d'hôte here is three o'clock.

The walk is occupied by the various drinkers as early as seven in the morning, and some of these patients will take 15 or 16 tumblers of saline and sulphurous water before 9 o'clock, the hour for breakfast. It really is marvellous to see what one individual can swallow on these occasions. In the evening a dance was proposed and a flute player sent for. Unfortunately however, he could neither play in time nor in tune, and Miss Lloyd asked me if my manservant could play upon her brother's flute. I sent for Edmund, and he very soon played with ease upon it. We danced some quadrilles and country dances to his playing which was in good tune and time and taste. My partners were Miss Lloyd, Miss Rickman, Miss Smith and Mrs Hinde. Our ball was over by 11 o'clock. There was a Miss Evans of Swansea at the Inn who excelled in powers of conversation not of her sex. Travelling and politics formed her chief themes and she was a violent reformer.

Friday, September 23rd. Before eight o'clock this morning I went, glass in hand, to the Pump walk, but I only took two glasses of sulphur water and one of saline. Quite enough I perceive, by what I feel this evening – a headache and unpleasant fullness about the head is the result of this very small dose. Before taking the sulphur water regularly, patients are usually bled, a preparation that I perceived to be founded on experience. Yet if only two glasses of sulphur water can have this effect on me what must it have upon those who take a dozen of them! Maurice Lloyd this morning took one glass and brought it up again immediately, so he had no temptation to repeat the experiment.

After breakfast I left Llandrindod. The weather was rainy. Dined at Llanbadarn Fynydd and reached Pennarth 31 miles from Llandrindod about ½ past 4 in the afternoon. In this tour I was particularly struck by the strong resemblance between Llanidloes and Newtown, the same factories, the same river, the same bridge of three arches on the west side, the same kind of low roof on the adjoining church tower, the same scattered fir trees on the green hill to the north, the same style of cultivated hills in the distance towards Llangurig, the same sort of market place with low brick arches – in short, if Llanidloes had not furnished the model as to situation and style of building, I doubt whether Newtown would have existed in its present form. The chief eyesore in the neighbourhood of Llanidloes is a brown hill of sheep walks at the north-east of the town. Beyond there is a sheltered house belonging to Mr Meers. In the course of this excursion I have seen some splendid scenery, contrasted with a greater degree of desolation than I could have supposed hitherto to exist in Wales.'

John Parker

Chapter 13

The Journal – June-July, 1833

Parker's journals show that he had a keen eye for detail and although his tour through Snowdonia in June and July, 1833 was plagued by bad weather, he tenaciously proceeded with it and utilized his time to the best possible advantage to extend his knowledge of the area. It satisfied his artistic talents, enhanced his botanical interest and reinforced his strong Gothic beliefs. The satisfaction which he obtained from this particular tour is quite apparent from his journal:

Wednesday, June 19. Left Oswestry by 'Wonder' coach at 10 o'clock – inside – weather unsettled, reached Capel Curig at ½ past 4, dined. In afternoon chose a subject for tomorrow and made a vignette.

Thursday, June 20. Fine morning, after breakfast rain came on, sketched Moel Siabod from bedroom window, cleared up after twelve and went to my subject a ¼ mile from the Inn, a great stone in the foreground. At ½ past 2 dined and at about 5 o'clock overtaken on the road by 'Wonder' coach – went outside for 4½ miles, gave Coachman 1. 6d. alighted at Benglog Falls. Went along opposite side of Nant Ffrancon and got a fine subject, a cottage in the foreground, the falls in the middle distance, beyond them Trevaen and Glyder Fach, a red sunset. Mail passed by to Bangor at ½ past 8, returned on foot along Llyn Ogwen. In the twilight, selected a subject of Trevaen and the Glyder Fach with large rock in foreground, returned to Capel Curig at a quarter to 11 at night.

Friday, June 21. Rather a fine but very windy morning – turned out a decidedly rainy day, dined at half past one. Heard this evening the account of Mr Homer's death near Capel Curig last November. Mr Homer was considered as partially deranged and set out from his Hotel (the Inn at Capel Curig) with a Lieutenant . . . whom he quitted very shortly, saying that he should go to the summit of Moel Siabod. He borrowed a pair of gloves which were afterwards found on top of that mountain. As night came on, Mr Homer's absence caused some alarm at the Inn, and on the following days much anxiety was felt as to the cause of it. In the course of about a fortnight, however, his corpse was discovered under a shelving rock that is in sight of Llyn Gwynant, on the rugged slope above the lake. The weather had been foggy with snow, and his path was traced for some distance on Moel Siabod but his body was found by accident. The poor fellow did not seem to have received any outward injury but his death seemed rather to have arisen from cold and hunger. He could hardly have lost his way for the road was in sight and houses, I believe, in view, but he had collected from distant places heaps of rushes and fern with some stones and of these materials he had made a rude shelter in addition to the natural rock which overhung him. The body had not begun to decay, his feet were without his stockings and placed in his hat round which he had also bound a part of his coat, and every circumstance appeared unaccountably perplexing. Mr Homer had received a classical education and was the son of a Tutor at Rugby. His death I imagine to have been caused by eccentric and imprudent exposure to cold accompanied by a sudden fatal exhaustion. I also heard that an ancient grave at Gorphwysfa called Bryn y Bedd was opened in 1831 when a stone coffin was discovered containing a skeleton. Unluckily for the presumed antiquity of this tomb, a tinder box and tobacco pipe were found lying among the bones!

Saturday, June 22. A wet windy morning, dined early at ½ past 2. Set off by 'Wonder' coach for the Benglog Falls, left my pencil behind me but borrowed one from the Guard which I am to return on Monday. The weather became worse – took shelter under an overhanging rock from whence I saw the steeps of Glyder and Trevaen gradually veiled by clouds, until only the lower parts remained in sight, stayed there for 3 hours and as I could not go on with my subject while the clouds concealed it, I fell asleep. On waking found the weather still worse – walked back in the rain 5 miles to Capel Curig.

Sunday, June 23. In spite of the falling weather glass, today was fine. At 11 o'clock went to church. Mr Hughes of Capel Curig did the duty in Welsh. He has a loud voice. In the chancel windows are some fragments of ancient glass. After an early dinner, walked along the road with a tourist who was at the Inn. We went to the Calvinistic Methodist Meeting House where there was a prayer meeting but no preaching – I was sorry to see there a larger congregation than at the church.

Monday June 24. A wet and cloudy morning, dined early, went off in the 'Express' coach and alighted at Benglog – after sketching for half an hour, began to ascend to the Twll Du – met three tourist who had missed their way. One, a botanist, returned under my guidance to the Twll Du. We reached it in about an hour. Found there all the rare alpine flowers except the Anthericum. On getting to the top, I offered him the choice of two ways back, either the road, or over the Glyder Fawr, both about the same length but the latter, which we chose, is difficult. We ascended Glyder Fawr, the clouds beneath us but not by us, and a splendid sunset gilding all the shores of Anglesey. On the top of Glyder Fawr (the habitat of the Juniperus) we looked for some time for that plant and at last we supposed we found it but not in any quantity. The peaks of Snowdon were clouded but there was a good deal of sunshine. I suspect that some botanical robber has been despoiling The Glyder Fawr of its Juniper. Nothing could be finer than that view, but we were too late. The colouring was rather too pale – the sheaves of rock upon the platform were very singular and interesting. I took my companion along the Waen Oer, and we looked on the magnificent view to the right and left which nothing could be more splendid. I remember particularly, one gigantic overhanging precipice beneath which lay a vista of Nant Ffrancon and the winding of the Ogwen close by Port Penrhyn and Beaumaris. We then passed close under the platform of Glyder Fach and it became dark. The wearisome descent from hence to the road was more annoying than ever owing to the increasing darkness with only half a moon. I thought we never should have reached the road. At length, however, after tumbling over rocks, and splashing through bogs, we did reach the road and after some time we arrived at Capel Curig about ¼ past 11 o'clock.

Tuesday, June 25. After breakfast, Mr Darwell, whom I had guided over Glyder Fawr yesterday and his two friends were going to Llanberis and as my way as far as Snowdon was along the same road, they accompanied me. They were Cambridge men, and were well known to Professor Sedgewick who has lately been in North Wales, i.e. during the last two summers. He considered Snowdonia to be extremely perplexing as to Geology. Having left the 3 tourists I went up to Llyn Cwm Ffynnon and sat down opposite a fine collection of rocks, with Snowdon in the background, and this lake in the middle distance, with a small island in the corner of it. After spending an hour and a half in sketching I returned by a short footpath to the ale-house at Pen y Gwryd where they gave me some luncheon and then passed along the road to Capel Curig which I reached about half past seven to a late dinner.

Wednesday, June 26. Woke this morning about 6 o'clock with a dreadful headache, and was not much better after breakfast. Another tourist was laid up with a headache and sickness. The weather was beautiful – Snowdon entirely cloudless and the style of colouring beautifully dim and faint. Before dinner I re-examined my view of Snowdon from above the Holyhead road. At two o'clock, after an early dinner, I walked along the road and a short distance beyond the first milestone from Capel Curig followed a footpath which led me to a farmhouse beyond which I got a good subject – the Glyder Fach and Trevaen with Llyn Ogwen – but the weather became rainy so I took shelter below a hollow rock and returned when the rain ceased to Capel Curig without any sketch.

Thursday, June 27. Cloudy morning, the glass rather low but not a decidedly bad day. At 12, set off to Llyn Cowlyd which is not more than a mile and a half from Capel Curig, but the path is obscure and in some places quite invisible and on both sides are deep morasses. The view of Glyder and Trevaen from this upland moor is truly superb, especially where a part of Llyn Ogwen appears. Llyn Cowlyd, altho' not wide, is a lake of great length but of no interest. There seems to be no tree in any part of the shores and the dessert mountain descend into the water unbroken, and hardly a footpath on either side. I made one vignette of this lake not expecting to see it again. Then went on for about a mile under a mountain called Pen Llithrig y Wrach until I came in sight of Llyn Eigiau. I then returned and visited Llyn Geirionydd. On the shore of this lake it is reputed Taliesin resided and I felt anxious to examine the scene on which the eyes of that great poet so frequently rested. I descended a very steep cliff, the lower part of which appears so precipitous, that until I saw two men below in the act of ascending, I was doubtful whether I could accomplish it in safety. I crossed some marshy meadows and presently reached the shores of Llyn Geirionydd. This is a long water – marshy on one side, on the other overhung by an exceedingly grand precipice abruptly rising from it. Though this feature is grand, yet the shores of this lake are not picturesque. There is no wood and it is open to the North East. The neighbourhood of Taliesin's abode, was, I am sorry to say, less interesting that I could have desired. The ruins of his house are said to be still in existence but I could see no vestige of any ancient building, and the shore of the lake is on one side utterly barren, on the other it is flat and marshy. But in going towards Ffynnon Llyffant, the scenery although barren becomes romantic and picturesque. The frowning rocky steeps that overhang Ffynnon Llyffant, and the sheltered seclusion of the glen beneath it, would have been delightful in fine weather. I made a hurried vignette of this view from a cottage, and certainly felt an interest in the reflection that I was treading a footpath frequented by the great inventor of Welsh metre by one whom classical versification was not unknown. The Welsh bard in bearing witness to the fame of Aneurin has immortalized this neighbourhood and made it henceforth poetic for ever. And altho' that lake is now a barren spot, yet in the time of Taliesin the flat side of it might have been wooded, and the marshy part may have been deep water. The rocks in the immediate neighbourhood of Hafod y Rhiw abound in the Globeflower. I am so much attracted by the precipice of Ffynnon Llyffant that I shall try to go there at some future time. That alpine pool seems worthy to have been the favourite haunt of Taliesin. It lies under the summit of Carnedd Llewelyn the second highest of the Welsh mountains. I ascended the very steep rocks under Cefn Llithrig y Wrach and on reaching the top found that the wind, tho' still violent, was not so furious as in the morning. Clouds covered all the mountains and I trudged along through rocks and bogs for 2 miles till I descended into the Irish road. Then it began to rain heavily. The mail passed me at eight o'clock and I reached Capel Curig soon after, wet through in my feet, but otherwise not the worse for my day's labour. On entering the Coffee Room at Capel Curig, I found Dryden Corbett and three other men, one a great traveller, full of conversation and another young Irishman whose name was Vernon, the third I had not seen before.

Friday, June 28. Weather still unsettled – after breakfast wrote journal and tinted and retouched vignette etc. Settled bill for rather more than 9 days at Capel Curig, charges reasonable, breakfast 2s. dinner 2s. 6d., wine ½ pint sherry 1s. 6d. Coffee 1s. 6d. bed 2s. At half past two set off by 'Express' coach for Penrhyn Arms 13 miles, rather windy but not wet. Mountains clear. Passed Ogwen Bank and the slate quarries and arrived at Penrhyn Arms about 4 o'clock. Evening cold and rainy.

Saturday, June 29. Bad weather – constant showers, cold and noisy wind. Penrhyn Castle is now finished as to general outline and has become a grey colour so that it looks as old as Conway or Caernarvon – dined early – went twice into Bangor, in the morning to Shone's the

Booksellers where I bought 'The Cambrian Tourist', in the afternoon to evening service for which I was too late, it began at 3 o'clock, at the Inn they said it began at half past four.

Sunday, June 30. Weather still cold and showery, went to morning service at ½ past 11. The Welsh morning service in the Nave was not ended, the sermon was being preached, and there was a large congregation. When that was over the English Cathedral Service began in the Choir. Here also there was a large congregation. The responses and psalms were chanted but the rest of the service was only read. All of it except the Epistle was done by the Vicar Choral, Mr Cotton, who has a good voice and earnest manner – he preached a very good sermon dwelling much upon the duty of praying for the King – the anniversary of William the IVth's succession occurred on Wednesday last. The modern Gothic in the choir of this Cathedral is of the most odious and vulgar description. It is by far the worst attempt at the style that I ever saw.

Monday, July 1st. Windy rain and cold weather – after breakfast a party was going from the Inn to see Penrhyn Castle by ticket. Mrs Bicknell has three of these to dispose of every week, and all who can go take these opportunities. A Mr Turner and his lady were setting off with post horses and I went with them. Having seen Penrhyn Castle more than once before, the outside had no novelty for me but I was anxious to see how they have managed the Anglo-Saxon furniture in woodwork (Parker's first visit to Penrhyn Castle was in 1829). They have kept up this peculiar style in the windows, doors, walls, chimney pieces and ceilings, in the beds, chairs, tables, wardrobes and even to the door hinges. The oak woodwork is not varnished and will be suffered by slow degrees to become darker. The ceilings of plaster, are painted light oak, which as the real oak becomes darker, will betray itself I suppose. The drawing room is hung with silk, and the modern scroll foliage of the pattern seems rather to harmonize with the ornaments on the capitals of the pillars – these are lofty, purely Norman in style and the beadwork is gilt, the flat coved ceiling is groined, the spaces between each rib are painted light oak with stars of gilding. The doors although not rich are of massive oak and of good proportion, a chimney piece almost resembling a rock or marble owing to the massiveness of its design is surmounted by an immense looking-glass enclosed with Anglo-Norman patterns. The furniture of this room is in the same style. Very thick short pillars and Norman mouldings are the chief peculiarities and here and there foliage of later character is introduced, but in general, the style is preserved even to a painful exactness. The ceiling of a small room next to the drawing room is quite flat, but is painted stone colour, which has a bad effect. This apartment is called the Ebony Room for the furniture being of that material, with a good deal of black marble. The slate bed is groined in wood, the flat vault resting on Anglo-Norman pillars. Two ranges of Norman arches carved in wood form the head of the bed and some rich foliage is on the foot board. Between the elliptical arch of the vault and the curtain rod there is a kind of partly semi-circular spandrel, which I don't much admire but it cannot be well disposed with. All the furniture of this room is Anglo-Norman but the flat ceiling tho' in the same style does not harmonize with the vaulted bed. The chimney piece and full length glass are good specimens of adaptations to modern customs. A small chapel with painted glass and good Norman vaulting, semi-circular at the end, and well furnished with rich woodwork to correspond, appeared handsome and appropriate. Near to this was a groined passage of great beauty. The staircase, which is to communicate with the great hall is rather small, but of most sumptuous design and elaborate execution. All the decorative powers of style are being lavished upon this part of the building which is lighted by an Anglo-Norman rose window of plate glass forming a skylight in the centre of a square vault in plaster, and rather too full of ornament. This use of the circular window is rather a hazardous attempt and tho' it may seem fastidious to condemn it, I cannot help thinking that some secret principle of rib-vaulting is compromised by it. The unfinished part of Penrhyn Castle are now closed up from the rest by walls of brick and plaster to prevent the dust from spreading into it, a very needful precaution. We went round therefore, to the great hall which will be a most enormous collection of arcades and heavy Norman groining. It is lighted by windows and from skylights. The surrounding passages above and below and opening into it, are more pleasing than the hall is likely to be. I perceive that the Norman style pleases most where it approaches the higher elegance of the pure Gothic, and altho' this Castle when complete will exhibit a wonderful specimen of adherence to style, yet that style not being the best and the decorations acquiring beauty rather from their position than their own elegance of design, the eye will become satiated with forms that are essentially made in their conception. The last room that we examined was the Library. This by some bad management, has more of an Elizabethan air about it than rude Norman dignity. The ceiling is not only flat but low – very much covered with plaster foliage. There are massive piers in this room, enclosing chimneys. In one of the finished rooms I observed large pictures in modern gilt frames which appear rather out of character where all other things were so studiously harmonized.

We left the Castle by another road and passed through the Llandegai Lodge gate. This lodge was built before the Castle and is a very fine specimen of Norman style. The centre is occupied by two large arches with zig-zag mouldings and the space between them is groined with stone. The corners of the building are adorned with four small turrets resting chiefly on brackets, and a series of interesting arches over the entrance gateway are divided in the middle by a shield bearing the family motto.

After an early dinner I strolled into Bangor and entering the Cathedral made measurements and a sketch of the font, which is handsome of perpendicular date, and is now placed in the west end of the south aisle. Bishop Skeffington has the credit of having built this Cathedral in 1582, but I see many windows and two doors which belong to the Early Gothic and were evidently built soon after the reign of Edward the First, who was a great benefactor of this Bishopric. The side arches of the Nave and the roof are of Skeffington's building but there are two arches of earlier date. Bangor Cathedral is not handsome. The tower is exceedingly mean and the total absence of pinnacles in the body of the church gives it a low appearance. Went to the Watchmakers and had my watch mended, returned in the afternoon to the Penrhyn Arms. Weather still cold and unsettled.

Tuesday, July, 2. Today the weather seemed improving so I crossed at the Garth Point Ferry and walked on to Beaumaris about a mile and a half. Ordered dinner at the Buckley Arms. This new Inn commands a most superb view of Beaumaris Bay with a distant horizon of mountains, woody shores, building and shipping. Penrhyn Castle is in full view, and as the clouds rolled away I saw from afar each well known peak and precipice of the Glyders. Went into the Castle and got a ladder by which I reached the groining of the chapel and measured various parts of it, returned at 2 o'clock to dinner at the Inn. The view of Snowdonia from the Coffee Room is most enchanting, after dinner again in the chapel where I remained until half past five. Then went round the grounds of Baron Hill, Sir Richard Buckley's. The view, altho' not always fit for drawing, is of a delicious character. The range of Snowdonia rises at intervals through groves or single trees of tall growth, and the Bay of Beaumaris lies below. From some spots, the Castle and the church are seen. This very fine landscape reminds me of Inverary – but the Bay of Beaumaris far surpasses the dull wildness of Loch Fyne, yet both scenes have the same southern aspect, and the same rare combination of sea and woody shore. Passing the house which has no attraction beyond that of a good situation, I went in quest of Queen Joan's monument, and not having been there for some years I missed it, and walked over all the neighbourhood of the house, until after enquiry some passing stranger set me right.

I found the modern Gothic building which a few years ago sheltered the sarcophagus lying in fragments on the ground, while a couple of rustic arches in rough branch work were being put up instead of it. The inscription is in Welsh, English and Latin. It mentions that the coffin having been removed from Llanfaes Priory, was used for some time as a watering trough, that it once contained the remains of Joan wife of Llewelyn ap Iorwerth, Prince of Wales and daughter of John King of England, that she died in 1237 and that Lord Buckley removed the coffin to this place of safety in 1802. I returned in the rain to Beaumaris, paid the bill, set off to the Garth Point Ferry, crossed it and returned to the Penrhyn Arms at 9 o'clock after a somewhat interesting day.

Wednesday, July 3, Weather fine – after breakfast crossed the Garth Point Ferry and went along the way to the Menai Bridge, it was high water. Nothing could be more beautiful than these woody shores interspersed with villas and cottages, while three or four islands with much rock and some wood gave interest and variety to the landscape. Yet, I failed in getting these well and harmoniously combined within the scope of one subject, there was water, shipping, rock, wood, building, islands and a mountainous coast on the horizon – crossing the road on the Anglesey side of the Menai Bridge I followed a footpath which led me along a sort of embankment to the insular church of Llantysilio. This very small but elegant Gothic building is crowned at the west end by an open arch for a belfry, while its eastern window though not highly wrought, is well designed and of the 14th century. The inside contains no object of interest. The present font, a plain octagonal stone is placed upon an older one of the very same pattern. Returning to this place I made a drawing of the Menai Straits with Llantysilio church in the foreground – a picturesque and uncommon subject. In crossing the Menai Bridge I could not help remarking that the display of naked machinery however grand the scale, when it is not under the contact of strict architectural rules, fails to produce lasting admiration – an electric shock of wonder is felt by everyone when first passing over the Menai Bridge, a feeling that is never experienced on a second visit. The science of its construction may continue to delight the mechanic but it is no longer acknowledged as fine work of art. The eye requires to be satisfied. The principle of suspension is not only new but I doubt whether it can ever be rendered picturesque. The angles formed by the towers and the roadway have a strange and anomalous appearance. It would no doubt be an improvement it they were partially filled up with open iron work in some sort of curve so as to give the semblance of an arch. Gothic tracery would have been beautiful here but the Roman style, of having been adopted, that is now out of the question.

Several fine views of the bridge are met with on the Bangor Road all of which have been seized upon by the artist and published in copper plate or lithography. The naked angles at the junction of the roadway to the towers here also appear to be the grand objection. This produces an effect which in reality the eye does not comprehend and in a drawing it violates probability.

I returned through Bangor to the Penrhyn Arms, the dark blue sea of Beaumaris Bay was today very brilliant. After dinner I went to the Garth Point Ferry meaning to make a careful sketch of Penrhyn Castle etc. but although all the members of a splendid sketch were before me, I became fastidious, and thought they could be better combined. The wind was also very cold and I returned to the Inn and then walked on to the church of Llandegai about a mile from the Penrhyn Arms. This church is a decent building of second rate Gothic approached by an avenue of Yew Trees. The square central tower slated on the sides, does not look well. Inside are three monuments of interest and importance belonging to the Penrhyn family. The most ancient is of alabaster and is of Gothic date. The two recumbent figures, as large as life, represent Piers Griffith of Penrhyn and his wife – the figures are much injured and the inscription, probably of brass, does not remain – below is a range of small statues under crocketed canopies in alabaster. These are also much defaced. This monument is in the South transept. The second in order of time is that of Archbishop Williams who held the See of York in the time of Charles the First, and was also Lord Chancellor of England. The talents of this man were very great, but in the unhappy times, the Cambrian failing, a sacrifice of principle to personal feelings, induced him to desert the Royalist side in the siege of Conway, when he met with a severe accident. A Latin epitaph records his talents, his dignities and his misfortunes. The Archbishop is represented kneeling at an altar and in his robes, the figure somewhat smaller I imagine than life. The rest of the monument is in second rate Roman style of that period. The third and latest monument is to Lord and Lady Penrhyn. This is of white marble by Westmacott – above the central inscription are small groups of children – at the sides are two figures as large as life – one represents a Welsh peasant, a slate worker, the other a girl with a wreath of oak leaves on her head, both of them look at the inscription. The female figure is seated – the other standing – but these modern monuments, from not having any Gothic work on them, are out of character in a church, and do not harmonize with it. How magnificent these figures would be if they were enclosed in canopies of good Gothic.

John Parker

Chapter 14

A Memorable Journey – 1836

In September, 1836, John Parker made the journey from Llanmerewig to St David's in Pembrokeshire. It was a journey which left a profound impression upon him in many ways, and a journey which added considerably to his interest in Gothic architecture.

It was, however, a journey tinged with disappointment and anger. Having left Llanidloes, the road took him to Llangurig where he had to stop and examine once again the beautiful chancel screen which he had seen on a previous occasion. He went into the church –

'Alas! Alas! When I last saw it, the interior was wretchedly paved and miserably neglected, but then there was a fine old Font on steps in the centre of the west end and there was a chancel screen of most exquisite Gothic, highly wrought and well designed which although damaged, yet gave an ornamented and sacred character to the whole building. Instead, therefor, I find vulgar modern pews and the whole screen has been swept away – no vestige of it remaining. They say it was all rotten and fell to pieces by itself, they say it was used as fuel to eke out the turf in the village hearths, they say it was considered of no value even by the man who contracted for the new pewing and took all the old parts as part of the bargain. They say that these fragments of Gothic foliage and tracery were carried off, some here, some there, but all of them to destruction. Oh! what pearls we have cast before swine. What feeling for science, what refinement of taste has been displayed in the nineteenth century! This was all done a year ago, and it is considered 'a very great improvement'.

There was some consolation, however, because on his first visit in 1828 he had taken accurate measurements of the screen and had made a drawing of it which would at least proclaim its exceeding beauty. In 1840 he made yet another visit to Llangurig and on that occasion he learnt that the screen had been 'destroyed by some dissenting carpenters who were employed in removing it and took, I am told, a malicious delight in trampling on the fragments of it while, by so doing, they brought the church more upon a level with their own vile meeting houses'. This was one of the few occasions when he vented his feelings against the Dissenters.

It was always a cause of surprise to him to find elaborate pieces of Gothic woodwork in such a church as Llangurig, but he had no doubt that such screens had been placed in such unsightly churches and that there had always been the glaring contrast between them and the 'shapeless barns' in which they had been constructed.

His journey took him through Devil's Bridge where there was an opportunity for him to make a hurried sketch of the road leading to Hafod – one of the most notable mansions of Wales in its heyday. He had already visited the house a few years earlier.

From amongst the lush woods of Pontrhydfendigaid he saw Ystrad Fflur (Strata Florida) the most noted but least visited of all the Welsh Abbeys in Parker's day. His visit here had a profound influence upon him and in his Journal we find not the words of the curious traveller but we read the expressions of a man who was able to identify with what had taken place there all those centuries ago. He looked upon the picturesque scene with more than ordinary interest because of his conviction that the Abbey had been the only monastery which had devoted itself to the wholesome preservation of national feeling by impartially putting on record the 'troublesome politics of the day'. And it was here, if anywhere, he reflected, that 'the peculiarities of the British church must have persisted and their apostolic origins acknowledged'.

With these thoughts lingering in his mind, he rose earlier than usual the next morning and made his way, with a guide, to visit the ruins. The magnificent western doorway was almost entirely concealed by trees and bushes and would not have received much attention from a casual visitor, despite the fact that a specimen of Norman style of greater elegance could not be found anywhere. Nothing was more pleasing to him than to find the mid-day sun throwing exquisite shadows upon the deeply recessed entrance where 'the Gothic principle is developed so perfectly here that the Roman architect must confess himself to have been surpassed even in the treatment of his own round arch'.

Here, he longed to linger –

' . . . about this inviting spot, interesting alike to the historian, to the painter and the poet. Here in times of warlike violence dwelt the man of learning and the man of taste. He dwelt here who scrutinized the mysterious dealing of God with a Celtic Nation; he who recorded amid the silence of contemplation the fall of heroes and the strivings of mighty men. Does not our knowledge that such mental efforts were made here, not invest us, as it were, with a degree of spiritual grandeur, the very soil that we are treading? He dwelt here who held with his hands the precious manuscripts, the ritual of the apostolic British Church. He dwelt here who wrought the freestone into forms of beauty, who clothed the dry skeletons of measurements with gracefulness of shape and colour.'

These are not the thoughts of the casual traveller, but rather the thoughts of a man who was in sympathy with the history of the place. They are the thoughts of the traveller, historian, painter and poet all embraced together.

When he eventually left Ystrad Fflur (Strata Florida) with the visions of what he had just experienced fresh in his mind, it was with disappointment that he viewed the church of Llanddewi Brefi. He expected much but his dreams were immediately dispelled by finding it to be one of the 'most vulgar rooms' he had ever seen. It did not even have the comforts of a modern room and it still retained its earth floor. Although the church had been recently repaired and two transepts leading from the side of the tower had been demolished his main concern was 'alas, that our alterations of Churches have preceded our improvement in taste'.

On his way to Lampeter he stopped at Llanfair Clydogau. Extremely small churches always held a certain charm for him and he would have found the church at Llanfair Clydogau picturesque had it not been grossly whitewashed consistent with the then current fashion. The interior, however, was dark and forbidding with a timber roof which appeared much neglected but when he recalled what had been done by improvements in other churches perhaps there was a chance after all that such neglect would not entirely destroy it!

It was Sunday when he arrived at Lampeter and he attended morning service which was partly in Welsh and partly in English. This church again was not in good repair and had a neglected appearance about it.

The view along the Vale of the Teifi was pleasing and picturesque, but his sights were now on Carmarthen where he began to be truly conscious of the fact that he was in South Wales, with its soft air and increasing warmth giving him the impression of Spring rather than Autumn. The new church on the outskirts of the town pleased him but he was disenchanted with the monument erected in honour of General Picton. The fame of Picton had outlived his monument – 'it is nothing more than the flimsy weakness of that composition sculpture which will not last any longer than it should last'.

After leaving Carmarthen, nothing excites him much but his thoughts were already on St David's and like Wyndham before him, he found the approach utterly devoid of interest or grandeur. No church tower was to be seen and the few houses that he saw had white roofs 'as if covered with eternal snow'.

Parker was to spend five days at St David's in awe and admiration of all that he saw. It was an experience which enriched his life and gave him another opportunity to enjoy the magnificent Gothic architecture which meant so much to him, and it complemented the experience which he had earlier enjoyed at Ystrad Fflur (Strata Florida). He did not dwell upon the dreariness of the place like Wyndham, to him, everything faded into insignificance when he surveyed the Gothic art that was all around him. His initial comments are interesting:

'How overpowering is the change of scene when the stranger descends the hill on which the village is built, and the grey Cathedral with the adjoining ruins, rising as it were, beneath his feet. Nor is the main wonder of that scene the external. I entered the Nave and stood in silent admiration. The vast arcade of Norman Gothic, the roof so highly wrought, so exquisitely harmonized with the walls, the ruinous but masterly Rood loft, all these had their effect in my first view. But I proceeded into the Choir under a doorway of skeleton vaulting in stone so beautiful, so rare in its design, that I paused for some time before I passed it. In the Choir I found ancient seats with rich finials, an episcopal throne, superbly conceived, over the altar three early Gothic arches once richly painted and under the central tower, a vault of Gothic woodwork.'

He does, however, share one curious view with Wyndham when he writes 'The Irish oak of which this grand ceiling has been constructed is never defiled by a cobweb, for no spider will come near any woodwork the materials of which have been grown upon the soil of Erin'.

His first view of St David's Cathedral was a time for contemplation and wonder and not for drawing – that would come later when he would return to examine and describe it in detail. Such was his first impression of this remote Cathedral, the retreat of ancient holiness and learning. It was to these qualities and the emotions connected with them that he ascribed the peculiar care with which men of wealth and science had adorned this corner of South Wales and that they had acquired a team of craftsmen who were able to undertake the work.

He returned the following day. It had rained all night and clouds of sultry warmth were floating around the walls of the Cathedral giving it an ethereal appearance. Here he contemplated upon the ancient Saints and scholars who had been there, and he would hear them speak of sacred things and of the independence of the primitive British Church who had considered Rome as an auxiliary but not a ruler. 'I can hardly tell why, but with all its deficiencies this place fascinates me exceedingly'. It was this fascination which enabled him to gain an understanding of the place and to identify himself with it so much.

He wandered up and down the Cathedral completely subdued by it and incapable of transferring any part of it to paper. The years rolled away and he became totally engrossed in the marvels of the fourteenth century.

It is difficult to highlight any single artefact which gave him the greatest pleasure, but the ceiling of the Nave particularly pleased him, and he wrote in his Journal:

'At evening, the sun burst forth and lighted up the vast Norman arcade while the solemn roof above, with its rows of pendants and their delicate foliage, retired away into the darkness of the central vault. I never beheld a grander scene, as to effect of light and shade combined with architectural richness. Let us describe it more exactly. Twenty six highly wrought pendants are suspended in two rows from one end of the Nave to the other, as many corresponding brackets unite the open arches of the wall. Three of the pendant arches cross the Nave, they are equal in height and width, accordingly this grand ceiling is all disposed under a tie-beam. But the arches altho' flat are not four-centred arches of the Tudor Gothic, but the depressed arch of two centres common in the fourteenth century. Between them the ceiling is arranged in squares, panelled alternatively transversely and lengthways. It will be said how could the architect endure to suspend his rich ornaments on a flat ceiling? I answer – this roof was once groined in stone, the arcades underneath began to lean outwards, the stone vault was removed, a tie-beam was found essential, and the wise Gothic Master-builder triumphed over difficulties by designing the present ceiling. Not but it could be had, I might prefer the complete arch, but I am a moderate man, if you give me the sublime, I am contended with it.'

That would appear to have been his ethos insofar as his predilection to Gothic architecture was concerned – he expected the sublime and the perfect.

Whilst Thomas Pennant provided the most comprehensive volumes on tours in North Wales, it was Benjamin Heath Malkin who was to provide the corresponding volumes for South Wales. In 1803 he toured the area and published his account in 1804, but the second edition entitled *The Scenery, Antiquities and Biography of South Wales* published in 1807 is the better known. He also provided a comprehensive account of St David's Cathedral, but in his Journal, Parker exhibits much more enthusiasm for the place and in so doing created a more vivid account, and his enthusiasm becomes contagious.

When the time came for him to renovate his church at Llanyblodwel it was to this particular visit to St David's Cathedral that he turned for inspiration in designing the ceiling with its squared panels and bosses with their corner patterns painted in similar colours to the true Gothic style. It is difficult to appreciate that the architectural styles from St David's Cathedral could be adapted to a small rural parish church like Llanyblodwel but he has been able to effect it and still give the church the lightness and richness which he admired so much. He had previously renovated the church at Llanmerewig again with ideas gleaned from the Cathedral.

Sunday was a day of rest from drawing so he wandered along the sea shore and found the transition from the magnificence of a Gothic Cathedral to the solitary scenes that were within a stone's throw of it most impressive. In the evening he went again to the Cathedral whilst the Welsh service was being performed and before the English service had begun.

A wedding was taking place at the Cathedral when he returned on the Monday morning to complete his drawing and it did not escape his notice that the service was somewhat different to that which he was accustomed to in that after the service began, the parties proceeded into the choir and the altar – 'a primitive custom' which he thought deserved the attention of English clergymen.

It was on Wednesday, 28th of September, that he left St David's but not before paying a final visit to the Cathedral, and once again we see him deep in contemplation when he wrote:

'While I gaze upon a scene such as this, my soul overflows with meditation. I recall past ages of the Christian Church and strive to separate their Godliness from their superstition. Amidst all that labyrinth of perplexing error I recognize the forbearance of God, the corruptions of the present age differ more in their nature than in their extent from those of earlier times, and where an apostolic church like ours has been either neglected or insulted, it is folly to sing the praises of our modern Christianity. From the fifth to the fifteenth century this Cathedral enjoyed a high degree of scholastic and religious welfare. For at least a thousand years it retained the light of learning.'

Most of the travellers through South Wales would have been to St David's and have almost without exception described the neglect and decay which they witnessed. They described the dilapidated and ivy-covered walls and the broken arches as if that was all that remained to exhibit the former extent and splendour of this religious establishment. This Cathedral, built on the site of St David's early monastic foundation soon evolved into a centre of pilgrimage and in the thirteenth century Pope Callixtus decreed that two pilgrimages to St David's equalled one to Rome – and it has been a centre of pilgrimage ever since.

Parker acknowledged the deficiencies which he saw but he also had a more constructive viewpoint and was able to see through those defects. In some respects, the defects served to highlight the splendour of the Cathedral to him, and whilst his views may well have been prejudiced by his penchant for Gothic art and architecture, he has left us with a very vivid account of the Cathedral as it was in 1836. He has also left us a remarkable and masterly water-colour showing the interior of the Nave with its magnificent ceiling.

His journey to Ystrad Fflur (Strata Florida) and St David's, two of the most important sites in the religious life of Wales, had been a memorable journey indeed, and one which left an indelible impression upon him.

Chapter 15

South Wales and the Border Counties

Although North Wales had a special attraction for Parker because of its wild and varied scenery, South Wales was not without its appeal to him. Most of his journeys to that part of the country are generally referred to as 'Gothic Tours' because he was always searching out for any sign of Gothic styles which he expected to find in the various churches – there was always something new to be found despite the fact that he had already visited some of the churches on previous occasions.

Following his tour in August and September, 1843, he wrote:

'Never within the same period of time have I added so largely to my architectural experience. Yet in the course of my whole tour I have seen only three new churches at Newport, Cardiff and Treforest, but I have hardly seen one of the many ancient ones that I have entered, which was kept in decent order, certainly not one that was well furnished or adorned. There appears a general absence of ecclesiastical taste and feeling.'

Once again he is expressing his own feelings and echoing the feelings of many other travellers who had toured the area before him. It is also interesting to note how his own feelings were changing when he expressed disappointment after revisiting a particular church after a long interval:

' . . . but I must remember that within the last 10 years, the public taste in church matters has improved rapidly, my own taste has been very much confirmed and I have been able to execute some exceedingly rich work both in wood and stone at Llanmerewig and at Oswestry. Now, therefore, of course rich ornament no longer appears to me so unattainable as it once did.'

Here again he acknowledges that each of his tours added to his knowledge and understanding of Gothic art, and more significantly, it reaffirmed his own strong convictions on the subject.

On this particular tour in 1843 he had crossed the border into Herefordshire and followed the Golden Valley through Vowchurch where he found nothing of any great interest in the little church with its pigeon house belfry. His destination was Dore Abbey, but as it was getting dark and he could only see its outline, he went in search of accommodation for the night.

Dore Abbey has been founded by French Monks in 1147 and is the only Cistercian Abbey which is still in use today as a parish church. The Abbey once owned large areas of land in the Golden Valley and its wealth came from sheep farming. The present church was formed in the restorations of 1630-1640 and 1701-1710 from the Presbytery, Ambulatory, and Transepts of the original Abbey.

He had been informed that the Abbey contained a wealth of carved work and so it was with renewed expectation that he went the following morning:

'and soon came in sight of the noble edifice, a fragment indeed of a larger building yet of sufficient loftiness to give it an air of grandeur. On first entering, the bleak walls and plain ceiling disappointed me, but on passing a screen of Elizabethan style, I beheld with astonishment the magnificence of the Gothic scenery that enclosed the altar. The style is of Early English but probably the richest of its date . . . I measured the altar stone. A farmer of the neighbourhood, now buried in the church, once removed this stone to his own house, and used it for salting bacon on, and it is a local tradition that it required a great strength of horses to take it there, whereas only two drew it back with perfect ease. I do not laugh at such reports, if they prove nothing else, they at least prove that sacrilege is regarded by the common people as being aided in some special manner.

I returned to the Abbey the following day and became familiar with its variety of ornaments and got through a great deal of architectural drawings. When I was left alone, I offered up some prayers before the altar. The north transept of this church has on its gable a cross resembling in its outline that on my belfry at Llanmerewig but it does not seem to be either gouged or bevelled. The whole of the stone work is defaced by repeated coats of white wash. In the shafts, this vile daubing does no harm except as to colour, but in the delicate foliage of the capitals it obliterates much of the beadwork and almost all of the most gradual changes of contour by which alone the artist is to be distinguished from the mechanic.'

Most travellers seem to have had a dispassionate outlook on the scenes around them and very few have given us more than a superficial account of what they saw, and fewer still had the inclination or the interest to describe in detail the various buildings which they passed with hardly a glance. Parker, on the other hand, had the propensity and the knowledge, not only to describe the buildings in detail but to impart his own feelings and philosophy when he came face to face with a particular building which had been allowed to fall into disrepair with uncompromising disregard to its importance.

It was but a short journey from Dore Abbey to Llanthony and his visit to Llanthony Abbey gives a clear demonstration of his feeling when he saw this once grand monastic church. Although much destroyed by time and man, the union of majestic and sacred art with the rich cultivation and all the wildness of nature impressed him. As an artist he could admire the romantic and picturesque scene of the ruined Abbey church set against the shadowy mountains covered with bilberries and heather but as a priest:

'although not a Romish one, I cannot behold the Temple of God in ruins without pain and sorrow. No 'pictorial effect' (as the newspapers would say) can compensate for the absence of worship or atone for the crime of sacrilege. Every monastic ruin bears witness against the sins of those who destroyed His place of worship.'

He could not help but be impressed with the west entrance and nave and side aisle of the Abbey which were probably the finest parts of the building and the west end with its two corner towers and enrichments of that beautiful transition style between Norman and Early English which he admired so much. All this, however, was marred when he visited an adjoining house belonging to a Mr Landor, the absentee landlord of Llanthony, and noticed that the materials used in its building had been obtained not only from the quarry which was nearby but also from the central tower of the Abbey.

When an earlier traveller visited the Abbey he found a modern door in one of the towers and on opening it found that it had been converted into a comfortable room, half parlour, half kitchen, with old arms suspended above the fireplace, and with sides of bacon flanking the white washed walls. Old chairs and cabinets and other items of furniture were also seen about the room, and he was offered tea by the occupant – the hospitality of the ancient monks was still in evident. It was here that the romantic poet Sothey years before had written:

'Here, was it stranger, that the patron saint
Of Cambria pass'd his age of penitence,
A solitary man, and here he made
His hermitage, the roots his food, his drink
Of Honddy's mountain stream . . . '

None of this would have impressed Parker. But he would have agreed with Giraldus' description of the Abbey in 1188, when he wrote:

'In the deep vale of Ewias, which is shut in on all sides by a circle of lofty mountains and which is no more than three arrow-shots in width, there stands the abbey church of St John the Baptist. It is roofed in with sheets of lead and built of squared stones, which are admirably suited to the nature of the place . . . It is a site most suited to the practice of religion and better chosen for canonical discipline than that of any of the other monasteries in the whole Island of Britain.'

Having satisfied himself with the architectural treasures which had been available to him, he returned to admire the landscape. From Llanthony Abbey he crossed the Black Mountains and went to Pont Nedd Fechan and visited the Porth yr Ogof Caverns. He found, however, that there were several small farmers extorting money from travellers to pass over their land. He wrote:

'One of them had the conscience to demand 2s. 6d. from Sir John Guest who had offered her 1s. for the passage of himself and Lady Charlotte. I gave 1½d. objecting to give more than I might have to pay for one horse at a common turnpike'.

Having paid, however, a further demand was made upon him when he came to a locked gate. This demand was also for a silver coin but he objected and only gave a penny – which did allow him access.

Parker, like all travellers to the area was intrigued by the Fall of the Hepste. His servant Evan rode his horse through the river near the falls while he walked underneath with his guide. He found himself on the other side with 'hardly a trace of spray upon my clothes or shoes, or any sign that I had been under water'. His fascination was such that he sent the guide back so that Evan could share the same experience.

He again met with disappointment at Brecon on the last stage of his return journey, for he found the Collegiate church a 'scene of mournful interest'. The fabric was so ruinous that services could not be held there. It contained the tombs and monuments of three Bishops, and he could not 'behold the desolation of their burial place without shedding tears.

The state of this building is a reproach to our National church and as a matter of deep humiliation to all her members who behold it. If it had been a dissenters meeting house, explained the man show showed it to me, it would have been repaired long ago, and I could not help feeling there was some truth in the bitterness of his remarks'.

It was market day at Brecon when he was there and the enclosure formed by the walls of the nave and side aisle of the church was, when he saw it, filled with horses. The streets were crowded with cattle and as he sat upon a wall near the church to make a drawing of it, cows and bullocks were almost jogging his elbow.

Many travellers of his time would have considered the tour as somewhat less than interesting but although he did experience disappointment more than once with what he saw, he could also recall other instances which had given him much satisfaction and led him to write that it was a tour which had added greatly to his architectural experiences.

Chapter 16

Caernarfonshire

The first recorded account of Parker's visits to North Wales was in 1819 when he was 21 years old, but subsequent accounts show that he was no stranger to the area even as a schoolboy. Once, when on the summit of Moel Siabod he recalled that the last time he was there was just before returning to Eton. The family had snatched a hasty tour of North Wales and found themselves on the brink of a precipice at seven o'clock on a fine evening but with mist all around them and the evening sun setting in a sea of blazing colour. Returning to Capel Curig they lost their way among the marshes and it was with some difficulty that they regained the proper path. Four days later he was back at Eton, his imagination full of the splendours of Snowdonia, and his noisy friends and school work making him yearn to be away. Much as he esteemed public schools in general he felt that there was an uncompassionate outward show of diligence about them that was both injurious and undignified.

The solitude of the mountains was later to give him ample opportunities for contemplation about his school days and his time at Oxford:

'And thou O! Oxford, once hated, now belov'd with what strange emotions do I recollect thee and with what regret? In thee, misunderstanding all ill-usage made me wretched, in thee also did I obtain thoughts more precious to me than health and riches. In thee did I meet disappointment, yet I cannot now dislike thee. Among these rocks indeed I should vainly seek for solemn chant, or columns and sacred arches, the melodious echoes of anthems, nor here can I meet the sweet elegance of youthful society. Still, here are charms peculiar to their kind, graces if they may be so called, of solitary nature and an awfulness of character influencing and probably exalting all beholders . . . I have passed through an University education at a time when English youth had begun to esteem wisdom and to purchase knowledge with real energy. Misfortunes indeed beset my path, yet I could not be unmindful of the public welfare and of the gradual improvement that was coming on. During my stay there from being almost loathsome to me, from appearing to be stained with endless vices, it assumed in my eyes at least a sacred character. O! that I had been able to contribute my share towards its future improvement. Yet I will not complain for providence ordains otherwise.'

The peace and tranquility which he found in the mountains gave him the opportunity to re-evaluate his life and afforded him the chance to be alone with his thoughts. Whilst he abhorred places where learning appeared to be inexorably tied to compulsion, he could express his own artistic and poetic feelings in the mountains of Snowdonia with impunity.

Much as he admired the mountains, Caernarfonshire had more to offer him, for here he could also appease his delight in Gothic art; it afforded everything that was important in his life.

In August, 1828, he spent some time in the Conwy Valley and visited the church at Llanrwst. As it happened, Bishop Luxemore was at Llanrwst for a confirmation service. It was Bishop Luxemore who had given him the living at Llanmerewig. This meeting with the Bishop had rather interfered with his plans because it had been his intention to start a drawing of the church but he could nor refuse the invitation to join the Bishop at the service. The church was crowded and the Bishop confirmed 'about 360 without any sign of exhaustion'.

When he was free to continue with his work he had the opportunity of examining the screen in some detail and found it more pleasing than any other he had seen. Unfortunately the body of the church was so dark that the rich ornaments were almost lost in shadow. The screen was not complete and he enquired of the Clerk whether he knew where the missing parts could be found, but the Clerk could not help him. He persevered and on looking over the church he found in a heap of dust under the floor of the Reading Desk two small pieces, one being the front of one of the larger canopies and the other one of the smaller canopies. He took these fragments with him to the Inn at Llanrwst where he was staying. This was to prove an embarrassment to him later!

The following day he went in search of the ancient Abbey of Maenan but found little evidence of its existence. The foundations of the abbey had been discovered a few years previously by Lord Newborough, the then owner of the land. This had been the original Cistercian Abbey of Aberconwy established in the last decade of the 12th century by the monks of Strata Florida in Cardiganshire. It was removed to Maenan by

Edward I in 1283 in order to make room for the building of his new castle at Conwy. The Abbey was demolished completely at the Dissolution and the timber and stones removed and used to repair the castle at Caernarfon.

Following the abortive visit to Maenan, he returned to the church at Llanrwst where he again met the Clerk and told him that he had found:

'several pieces of the screen in a heap of dust etc., two of which I took away to keep them. The fellow very gruffly told me I must bring them back. I said no more then but after an early dinner I sent for the Church Warden and showed him the fragments telling him the circumstances under which I had discovered them, and that they were of no value to any body, but a Gothic architect as they were broken and could not well be replaced, but that as models for working from they might be made useful. Mr Jones, the Church Warden was very civil and offered to do anything that was right and proposed to go with me to Mr Boulger the Curate – whom I said I should of course be willing to consult on this occasion. On our first calling at Mr Boulger's lodgings he was at dinner, afterwards we found him at home, and I laid the whole matter before him. The Clerk had been there before me and not having seen the fragments in question, had I suppose, left an impression on the mind of Mr Boulger that they were some large portions of the screen, for being perfectly prepared with his answer, he began by lamenting that his uncle, the Rector, was not in the country and that he was exceedingly particular that he would not suffer the smallest particle of the screen to be taken away, and that he Mr Boulger had no authority whatever to give, or to withhold anything, but that he should incur serious displeasure if it were known that he had consented to my proposal. I observed that nobody had more value for the screen than myself, that I should be the last person to wish to remove any part of it from the proper place, but that the case altered when I had brought to light some fragments of it, the existence of which was never suspected, which but for me, would never have been found, and which nobody in Llanrwst could restore to their original places. I also doubted the Rector's power over the screen (which I believe the parish might sell without his being able to prevent it). But, above all, I said if the Rector is this careful about the screen, why is it left in its present unsafe condition? One of the main beams on the western side has been half cut through to make way for a door and as twenty feet of it are thus left only half supported, the beam has bent inwards and the ornaments above it have all been distorted or destroyed.

However, it does not answer to make more stir about a thing than it is worth, and as I found that it was no use to plead 'right of trover' in this case, I quietly submitted to Mr Boulger's earnest request that I would have the fragments taken back to the church. It cannot be too generally known or acknowledged that altho' ancient works of Gothic art should ever be held sacred from the hands of covetous curiosity, still when fragments of them are discovered by those who understand their value, no impediment should be thrown in the way of their obtaining them. Drawings of the more minute or delicate ornaments of crockets for instance, are not sufficient as patterns for workmen. They must have a fragment of the thing itself or a model of it before they can equal the original. Unless this rule is well-known and acted upon, the progress of architectural science will be much obstructed, and may well have recourse to stealth in order to procure what should have been given them for the asking.'

If disappointment and embarrassment had been his experience at Llanrwst, he was sufficiently compensated when he travelled to Conwy to visit the parish church of St Mary. Here was a chancel screen which in its original state was one of the finest in North Wales but when viewed by Parker it 'had been much disfigured by modern work and is in a ruinous condition'. It was a screen of five arches filled with tracery with the ceiling enriched with panelling. The chancel screen, he considered to be 'a most rich example of the fan groining in wood such as may be seen in stonework at St George's Chapel, Windsor'. Some unsightly modern posts had been added because the organ had been placed in the gallery. Another traveller, Josh. Hawker, was in North Wales in August 1812 and he also confirmed that the screen supported the organ and added that the west door and the three windows above it were 'walled up by the Yahoos of Conway'. Parker made several drawings of the screen including a view of the screen and stall end looking west, a detailed drawing of the vaulting together with a side view from the ground.

The church also contains this memorial of Nicolas Hookes:

Here lyeth Ye Body of Nicks. Hookes of Conway Gent. Who was Ye 41 child of his Father WM. Hookes Esq., by Alice his Wife, and Ye Father of 27 children, who dyed Ye 20 Day of March 1637.

From Conway he returned to Llanrwst and settled his account at the Castle Hotel where the charges were considered exorbitant – 1s. 8d for a boy and 1s. 6d for a horse. He vowed to avoid this Inn in future.

Another tour took him to the Llŷn Peninsula, an area not much frequented by the early travellers.

Following a visit to the Castle at Caernarfon and the Llanbeblig and St Mary's churches in the town, his next port of call was Clynnog. When Leland visited Clynnog between 1536 and 1539 he stated that the old church where St Beuno lay was 'hard by the new church with cross aisles'. The monastery of St Beuno was founded early in the 7th century and was one of the two chief Sanctuaries in Arfon the other being Bangor. Adjoining the church and connected to it by a short passageway is St Beuno's Chapel. Pilgrimages to the saint's tomb were regular occurrences when the sick were brought to the tomb in the belief that they would be cured. Pennant gives the following account in his *Tours of Wales:*

'Votaries were wont to have great faith in him (St Beuno), and did not doubt but that by means of a night's lodgings on his tomb, a cure would be found for all diseases. It was customary to cover the tomb with rushes, and leave on till morning sick children, after making them first undergo ablution in the neighbouring holly well; and I myself once saw on it a feather bed, on which a poor paralytic from Meirionnyddshire had laid the whole night after undergoing the same ceremony.'

Parker, on the other hand, was much more practical in his accounts and only infrequently does he refer to such incidents.

The early Gothic screen was of interest to him and he made a number of drawings of it. He described the chancel screen as:

'Early Gothic arranged like that of Llanrwst but plainer – 8 arches with vaulting above and cornice border of Gothic foliage with hanging spandrels in flat arches, those connected with the piers being sharp lancets instead of tracery, they are adorned with a succession of rich foliation as also are the flat arches above them. Gresford and Wrexham are both very superior to Clynnog Fawr. The floor of the nave is remarkable to sloping from the transept towards the western tower, perhaps as much as two feet.'

It is recorded that 'devastating restorations' were carried out in 1856 when the majority of the old fittings including roofs disappeared but Parker had already recorded the screen in an undamaged condition. New parapets have also been added since then.

He left Clynnog on the Pwllheli Mail and visited Llanaelhaearn but there was very little in the landscape which held his attention, briefly he noticed Tre'r Ceiri and resolved to visit it on his return journey. At

Pwllheli he hired a car, a boy and a horse for 15s. for two days so that he could visit Llanengan. The church at Pwllheli had no appeal for him hidden away from sight as it was, and moreover, 'the Anabaptists abound here'. Travelling from Pwllheli towards Llanengan was tortuous but he found it more convenient and 'smoother over the sand of the ebbing tide'.

At Llanengan he found a substantial church with a conspicuous tower and two aisles. Having obtained lodgings at the Public House for himself, but no stabling for his horse, he went in search of the key for the church and commenced his drawings of the screens. The usual legend is attached to these screens, and in this case it is that their original home was Bardsey Abbey.

He returned again the following day, which was a Sunday, when he met the Rector. He was invited to stay at the Rectory and he sent his boy and the car back to Pwllheli. That evening he felt 'a violent cold coming on and took wine, whey and nitre'; it was his 32nd birthday.

For the next few days he was confined to his bed but managed to sketch the village and church from his bedroom window. His cold was better after a few days and he went with the Rector in a gig to Pwllheli and there they dined at the 'Crown and Anchor' Inn. After dinner he took the coach to Clynnog where he arrived at half past four and immediately went to the church to complete his drawings.

The following morning he again took the Pwllheli coach to Llanaelhaearn and went up to Tre'r Ceiri. There he enjoyed the magnificent views over the Llŷn Peninsula with the clouds rolling over him now and again and the sea beneath him a 'dark green, blue and purple with a rough appearance'.

His work in Llŷn completed he returned to Bangor expecting to return home the following morning but as there was no place inside the Express coach he deferred his departure until the next day. With time on his hands he took the Bishop's Ferry from Bangor to Anglesey and walked to Beaumaris.

Anglesey had suffered more than most counties in that more than half the churches have been rebuilt, demolished, abandoned or drastically improved. When Sir Stephen Glynn visited St Mary's Church, Beaumaris in 1848, he described the chancel as 'Perpendicular, and on each side are six wooden stalls surmounted by fine canopies and in the chancel is a fine alabaster tomb'. The church has since lost these fine canopies. Parker's comments on his visits are scarce, he described the alabaster tomb in the centre of the chancel and some old Gothic wood work in other parts but 'nothing of great value or beauty, arches dividing nave from the side aisle good Early English'.

Chapter 17

'Snowdonia' – A Gothic Poem

By 1859, Parker's health was deteriorating fast but he still wished to make a final visit to Snowdonia. In June, 1860 he persuaded his sister, Lady Mary Leighton and her daughter Margaret, to accompany him. It was with some reluctance that they agreed as Lady Leighton was aware of the difficulties posed by such a journey and the effect it would have upon her brother's failing health.

However, the party set out for Snowdonia and on the 21st June they went up Snowdon, but the mist prevented them seeing anything. A few days later they were on the banks of the river Glaslyn where Lady Leighton made a drawing of Beddgelert church which would form the first of her illustrations for 'Snowdonia'.

When they left Beddgelert, Parker was satisfied with the little that he had been able to accomplish but he was getting gradually weaker. Their journey home had to be delayed at Betws-y-coed and they had to remain there for a week until his doctor, who had been called from Oswestry, arrived to examine him. He was eventually allowed to continue his journey and he arrived home at Blodwel on the 2nd July. He died on the 13th August, 1860.

He had already completed his 'Gothic and Romantic Poem' entitled 'Snowdonia', and as a tribute to him, Lady Mary Leighton executed the folio sized illustrated version of the poem which is now in the National Library of Wales, Aberystwyth. Parker himself wrote the following preface to the work:

'SNOWDONIA is intended to be a specimen of a thoroughly Gothic and Romantic Poem grounded nevertheless upon strict adherence to the rules of the Greek metres. The illustrations which accompany the poem are drawn and coloured by my sister Lady Leighton. They represent copies of my own sketches, extending over a period of nearly half a century, during which time as a thoroughbred mountaineer, I became familiar with all the wildest localities of Snowdonia.'

Each page is accompanied by a detailed description by Parker of the actual location of the scenes and the circumstances upon which they were painted. These were taken from his original Journals. The poem demonstrates the affection which he had for Wales and outlines the country's violent episodes from its earliest beginnings. The first strophe and antistrophe describe his own personal delight and enjoyment:

Strophe I

Thou lonely but fertile valley!
With new delight I turn to thy shaded bowers
And rode along some green valley
That leads aloft among the wild fruit and flowers,
O! tranquil scene, happy wilderness
Bear me to thy grove, to the mountains rave,
Or let me abide in thoughtfulness
Near the hollow bank of the torrent wave!
That it is to repose on the higher ground of Poetic Wales
When dewy perfumes are wafted around
From the summer vales.

Antistrophe I

O! let me enjoy at leisure
The land of Alpine dreams, the Bardic environs
Where each lay of Celtic measure
Breath'd on the surrounding gale of the high poet's visions!
Thou gleaming abode of Druidic songs
To the latest age their spirit is thine,
Where the hurried wave so fiercely dashes
Down the rock of spray
Where the ray of noon so brightly flashes
Let me ever stay.

He is buried in a Gothic tomb in the shadow of his church with its unique tower at Llanyblodwel to which he had given so freely of his energy and endowed with so much of his expertise of Gothic art.

The following words are inscribed upon his tombstone:

To the/Sacred memory/of John Parker, died August 13 1860/
Vicar of Blodwel/He departed from us/at 61 years old/But his work remains.

His work will always remain as a fitting tribute to a remarkable man, but perhaps the most appropriate way to end this account of the Reverend John Parker, a resolute traveller and lover of Wales and Gothic art, is best declared by himself in the last Epode of his poem:

From the vale of breathing vapours,
From the lake of glassy wave.
So beloved of all beholders
From the Cromlech and the cave,
I depart, yet while departing
My reluctant eyes delay –
And tho' all the hills be dark'ning
    Hardly tear myself away!
Homely scenes and worldly fitness
Earthly cares and unquietness
Come to veil thy dreamy brightness,
    Those magic land of the lay!

John Parker's letter to 'The Builder' – 4th February, 1860.

Sir,

Architect's and Amateurs – The works at Blodwel.

A correspondent of 'The Builder', in a letter headed 'Architects and Amateurs' dated December 3, 1859 (Page 797) had almost avowed that he writes with a strong feeling of professional jealousy against amateurs in general, and although as one of the latter class, I avoid controversial writing, yet as my name has been brought forward in an offensive manner by him, I shall on this occasion defend myself, with your permission, from the attack of my anonymous correspondent, whom I suppose, although unacquainted with him, to be a resident in this neighbourhood and apparently my personal enemy.

He declares himself to be a 'legitimate practitioner and judge of these matters'. I am surprised therefore, he is not aware that my Blodwel spire, is by any means, the first example of a convex outline, for Claythorpe in Lincolnshire (damaged by lightning Dec. 30, 1859 and somewhat incorrectly represented in the Illustrated London News, Jan. 11, 1860) and Fribourg Minster in Germany show the same construction, and I believe I could name several others, but where they are slightly convex in outline, the artist or engraver may not always have represented them correctly. The domical curvature of the Fribourg spire I ascertained myself from personal examination. When I built the Blodwel spire, I thought its rather unusual form would be likely to promote a fair discussion on the question as to whether the dome or the spire should be preferred for our highest architectural outlines. But small indeed must the experience of any one be, who does not recognize in my spire, the essential form of the German Fribourg, and in the window treatment of my octagonal tower an evident imitation of the well known example at Sedgeberrow. Never until now, that I am aware of, has it been a matter of reproach to a clergyman that he has turned his attention to architecture as a branch of knowledge connected with his profession.

If the school and master's house at Blodwel which I have built and paid for, are unlike the ordinary type of National Schools in other places, they are intentionally so, and I can still appeal to them as true specimens of English Gothic feeling, nor have I ever admitted the features of any other style to neutralize my treatment of pure Gothic.

I consider it our own appropriate, living style, ductile beyond all others, and in adapting it, I lay myself under stricter obligation than those who offer, with perfect indifference, to build in any style that may suit the caprice of their employer.

But how could I act otherwise than I have done? The professional architect after supplying ground plan elevation and working drawings etc., will hardly visit the site more frequently than twice in the twelve months, and I as an amateur, think it my business to be present there almost every day and no stone of any size is put into its place without my personal superintendence.

It after works of this kind have been carried out at my own cost I am to be reproached with virulence for daring to act in such a manner, and by professional assailants as submitted by his brethren, it lowers the standard of practice throughout all departments of the profession.

My opponent refers to a hundred others but of whom he has done me the honour to select me for his first victim. The course of a hundred letters duly printed in 'The Builder' will no doubt annihilate the volunteer corps and we shall be forbidden ever after to express our practical opinions otherwise than on paper unless we are willing to brave all the bitterness of reproach – calumny.

However, before I am utterly destroyed, I have one appeal to make. I appeal not to the architectural world – at present so hopelessly divided between the contending styles – but I do appeal to the Gothic world, which is at unity with itself and the living, native, and growing style, now passing under that name, and is the only one I care to practice or am anxious to see employed by others.

In conclusion, Mr Editor, I cannot avoid observing that I consider your correspondent's 'threatening letter' as a very dangerous precedent. Perhaps even his professional exclusiveness might allow the Deans of our Cathedrals a legitimate voice in the disposal of their 'fabric money', and he will perceive by my signature to this letter, that I also have some official excuse for meddling with matters of architectural and Parochial expenditure.

John Parker,
Vicar of Blodwel and Rural Dean of Llangollen.

Jan. 7 1860.

Selection of John Parker's Tours and Excursions with main centres of interest

September 1819	Llanberis, Beddgelert, Rhaeadr Ddu, Hugh Llwyd's Pulpit, Dinas Emrys.
June 1820	Ffestiniog, Barmouth, Dolgellau, Llanelltyd, Tremadog. Beddgelert, Rhyd-ddu, Llyn y Dywarchen, Caernarfon, Bangor, Conwy.
June 1820	Capel Curig, Llyn Llydaw, Llyn Glas, Llanberis.
September, 1821	Welshpool, Llanfair, Llanerfyl, Cann Office, Mallwyd, Dolgellau, Barmouth, Cors y Gedol Nannau, Eaton Hall.
August 1822	Cernioge, Betws-y-coed, Capel Curig, Moel Siabod.
June/July 1823	Dolgellau, Bodowen (Barmouth) Vale of Ffestiniog. Tanybwlch, Llanuwchllyn, Llanfrothen, Beddgelert, Dinas Emrys.
July 1824	Capel Curig, Glyder Fawr, Glyder Fach.
June 1826	Betws-y-coed and Llyn Elsi.
February, 1828	Llanbadarn Fynydd and Abbey of Cwm Hir.
July 1828	Llangurig and Llanidloes.
September 1828	Llanbadarn Fynydd and Llananno.
September 1828	Llananno.
September/October 1829	Llanrwst, Gwydir Chapel, Maenan, Conwy, Bangor, Caernarfon, Clynnog, Llanaealhaearn, Abersoch, Llanengan, Pwllheli, Tre'r Ceiri, Penrhyn Castle.
April 1830	Bugeildy
May 1830	Radnorshire
March 1831	Montgomeryshire
August 1831	Ludlow, Hereford, Monmouth
September 1831	Llanidloes, Eisteddfa Gerrig, Ponterwyd, Devil's Bridge, Hafod, Pen Rhiw Wen, Rhaeadr, Cwm Elan, Llanbadarn Fawr, Llandrindod Wells.

September 1831	Llangollen, Plas Newydd, Capel Curig, Beddgelert, Nant Gwynant.
June 1832	Capel Curig, Glyder Fawr, Glyder Fach, Maen Du'r Arddu, Penllyn, Llanberis, Cwm Glas, Twll Du, Caernarfon, Llanrug, Carreg y Bardd, Llyn Du.
July 1832	Corwen, Capel Curig, Glyder Fach, Penygwryd, Cwm Dyli, Nant Gwynant, Llyn Cwm Ffynnon, Llanberis, Cwm Brwynog, Llyn Ffynnon y Gwas, Llyn Coch.
September 1832	St Asaph, Ruthin, Ellesmere.
September 1832	Llanrhaeadr.
October 1832	Mold.
June 1833	Capel Curig, Gorffwysfa, Glyder Fach, Llyn Eigiau, Hafod y Rhiw, Llyn Llyffant, Penrhyn Castle, Beaumaris, Menai Bridge, Llandegai.
September 1836	Llanidloes, Llangurig, Devil's Bridge, Hafod, Pontrhydfendigaid, Ystrad Fflur, Llanddewi Brefi, Llanfair Clydogau, Lampeter, Llanybydder, Carmarthen, St Clear, Haverfordwest, Roche Castle, St David's.
April 1838	Llansilyn, Glasgoed.
May 1840	Llanwnog, Carno, Talerddig, Llanwrin, Penegoes, Machynlleth, Talyllyn, Esgair Geiliog, Craig Goch, Cader Idris, Llanegryn, Clarach, Eisteddfa Gerrig, Llangurig, Llanddewi Ystradenni.
August 1840	Bala, Corwen.
August 1841	Bishop's Castle, Leintwardine, Lydbury. Brampton Bryan, Presteign, Stowe Hill, Knighton, Bleddfa, Llanfihangel Rhydithon, Penybont, Llananno, Llanbadarn Fynydd.
September 1843	Llanthony Abbey, Pont Nedd Fechan, Brecon, Golden Valley, Vowchurch, Abbey Dore, Caerphilly, Pontypridd, Grosmont.
August 1846	Llanfyllin, Garthribo, Llanelltyd, Pistyll Cain, Cader Idris, Arthog, Craig Aderyn, Towyn, Llangower, Rhiwedog, Bala.
August 1847	North Wales Tour.
October 1855	Penybont Fawr.
1826	Killarney.

| June 1829 | Netherlands, Germany, Switzerland, North of Italy, France. |
| June 1857 | London to inspect the progress of the building of the new House of Commons with W. Wynne, Esq., M.P. |

Glossary of Technical Terms

Ambulatory – processional aisle circling apse.

Apse – semi-circular or polygonal end to chancel.

Arcading – range of arches supported by piers or columns.

Boss – ornamental cover of join in rib-vaulting.

Campanile – attached bell tower.

Canopy work – any projecting cover over an altar, niche or other object.

Capital – head of column.

Chancel – portion of church east of crossing.

Choir – central portion of chancel where service is sung.

Clerestory – windowed top storey above aisle roof.

Clustered column –A pier which appears to consist of several columns or shafts clustered together.

Corbel – supportive block of stone projecting from a wall.

Cornice – top section of entablature – that is horizontal topping of columns.

Crockets – leaf shaped decoration on sides of spires etc.

Cusps – projecting point in Gothic tracery.

Decorated – English Gothic style c. 1280-1350.

Dog tooth – diagonal pyramid patterning.

Early English – English Gothic style c. 1190-1290.

Fan tracery – elaborate geometrical carved work which spreads over the surface of a vaulting, rising from a corbel and diverging like the folds of a fan.

Fan vault – where all ribs have the same curve and diverge equally in every direction.

Finials – top ornament of a pinnacle or gable generally used together with crockets.

Fluting – vertical channels on columns.

Foliated – leaf shaped carving.

Fretwork – perforated ornamental work.

Frieze – any horizontal band filled with ornament.

Groin – the edge where two faces of vault meet.

Lancet – tall narrow window, characteristic of Early English.

Light – the openings between the mullions of a screen or window, or sometimes named bays in a screen.

Moulding – contours around projecting features, windows, arches etc.

Mullions – vertical posts dividing windows into lights.

Nave – part of the church west of crossing for the lay congregation.

Pediment – low pitched gable above doors or windows.

Pendant – elongated boss.

Perpendicular – English Gothic style c. 1350's - c.1530's.

Pier – main support for arcade.

Pilaster – decorative pier attached to a wall.

Pinnacle – upright ornament on spire or tower.

Poppy head – the carved ornament placed upon the top of a bench or stall end.

Presbytery – area of high altar, east of the choir, also called sanctuary.

Quatrefoil – a panel divided into four by feathering, either circular or square in shape, having a small boss or shield in centre.

Rib vaulting – vaulting having ribs projecting below the general surface of the ceiling to strengthen and ornament it.

Rood – A crucifix with attendant figures of Mary and John. Rood beams used to support these figures.

Reredos – backing of high altar.

Rood screen – partition in front of nave, usually supporting cross or rood above.

Sanctuary – area of high altar.

Screen – separates the choir or chancel from the nave.

Spandrel – the triangular timber between the post and beam of a screen forming a curved brace, often enriched with carving.

Tracery – the ornamental perforated filling placed in the head of a light of a screen or in a window.

Transept – transverse arms of cruciform church.

Bibliography

Aikin, Arthur, *A Journal of a Tour through North Wales and parts of Shropshire.* (London 1797).

(By a Barrister), *A Tour in Quest of Genealogy Through Several Parts of Wales, in a series of Letters.* (London 1811).

Bell, David, *The Artist in Wales* (London 1957).

Bingley, William, *North Wales, including its Scenery, Antiquities, Customs etc.* (London 1804).

Borrow, George, *Wild Wales*, (Collins n.d.).

Cambrian Register, 1796.

Carr, H.R.C. & Lister, G.A., *The Mountains of Snowdonia*, (London 1948).

Catherall, William, *Wanderings in North Wales* (London 1851).

Cliffe, John Henry, *Notes and Recollections of an Angler* (London 1870).

Craddock, Joseph, *Letters from Snowdon* (London 1770).

Cumberland, George, *An Attempt to Describe Hafod* (Reprint, Hafod Trust 1996).

Defoe, Daniel, *A Tour through England and Wales* (2 vols. Everyman, 1948).

De Quincy, Thomas, *The Confessions of An English Opium-Eater* (World Classics, London 1902).

Evans, John, *Letters on a Tour of Wales* (1798).

Fenton, Richard, *Tours in Wales 1804-1813* Ed. John Fisher, London 1917.

Geraldus Cambrensis, *The Journey Through Wales and the Description of Wales* (Penguin Classics 1978).

Hoare, Sir Richard Colt, *The Journeys of Sir Richard Colt Hoare Through Wales and England 1793-1810*, (Ed. W.M. Thompson) (Alan Sutton, 1983).

Hucks, Joseph, *A Pedestrian Tour Through North Wales in a Series of Letters*, (Eds. Alun R. Jones and William Tydeman, Cardiff, 1979).

Hughes, W.J., *Wales and the Welsh in English Literature* (London 1924).

Hutton, William, *Remarks Upon North Wales* (Birmingham 1803).

Hyde Hall, Edmund, *A Description of Caernarvonshire (1809-1811)*, Caernarfonshire Historical Society, 1952).

Inglis-Jones, Elisabeth, *Peacocks in Paradise*, (Gomer Press, 1990).

Malkin, Benjamin Heath, *The Scenery, Antiquities and Biography of South Wales*, (London 1804).

Newell, R.H., *Letters on the Scenery of Wales* (London 1821).

Parker John, *The Passengers, containing the Celtic Annals* (London 1831).

Parry, Edgar W., *Y Teithwyr yng Nghymru (1750-1850).* (Gwasg Carreg Gwalch, 1995).

Pennant, Thomas, *Tours in Wales* (London 1784).

Pugh, Edward, *Cambria Depicta* (London 1816).

Rodenburg, Julius, *An Autumn in Wales (1856)* Trans. William Linnard, (Cowbridge 1985).

Roscoe, Thomas, *Wanderings in North Wales* (London 1853).
Roscoe, Thomas, *Wanderings in South Wales* (n.d. c.1840).
Skrine, Henry, *Two Successive Tours Throughout the Whole of Wales in 1798* (London 1812).
Trevelyan, Marie, *Glimpses of Welsh Life and Character* (London 1893).
Turner, Thomas, *Narrative of a Journey Associated with a Fly through North Wales* (London, 1840).
Warner, Richard, *A Second Walk Through Wales in 1798* (Bath 1800).
Williams, Peter Bayley, *The Tourists Guide through the County of Caernarvon* (Caernarvon 1821).
Wyndham, N. Penrrudock, *A Gentleman's Tour through Monmouthshire and Wales in 1774.* (London 1775).

Other Sources

Revd John Parker's Journals in the National Library of Wales;

N.L.W.Mss. 16086C – Foreign Tours.
N.L.W.Mss. 18250B – A Gothic Tour, 1841.
N.L.W.Mss. 18251C – Commonplace Book.
N.L.W.Mss. 18252B – South Wales Tour 1831.
N.L.W.Mss. 18253B – South Wales Tour 1836.
N.L.W.Mss. 18255B – South Wales Tour 1843.
N.L.W.Mss. 18256C – Tours (Various)
N.L.W.Mss. 19382E – A Gothic Tour and Miscellaneous Notes.
Archaeologia Cambrensis – Various Volumes, in particular – 1903, 1943, 1944, 1945, 1946, 1947, 1949, 1959.

Mountaineering & Botany

The Complete Guide to Snowdon/Yr Wyddfa
– Robert Joes. PVC Cover; ISBN 0-86381-222-8; **£6.95**

The Lakes of Eryri
– Geraint Roberts. Wildlife, fishing and folklore enhances this book aimed at anyone who loves Snowdonia. PVC cover; 256 pp; ISBN 0-86381-338-0; **£8.90**

The Mountain Walker's Guide to Wales
– Colin Adams. A comprehensive guide to 100 routes covering 200 Welsh peaks. 192 pp; ISBN 0-86381-154-X; Map, PVC Cover; **£6.90**

The Botanists and Guides of Snowdonia
– Dewi Jones. An account of the local guides and the plant hunters. 172 pp; ISBN 0-86381-383-6; **£6.95**

Travellers in Wales

Visitor's Delight
– Dewi Roberts. An anthology of visitor's impressions of North Wales. 152 pp; ISBN 0-86381-224-4; **£3.75**

The A-Z of Betws-y-coed
– Donald Shaw. Full of facts, stories and history about the popular Welsh resort. 136 pp; 0-86381-153-1; **£2.99**

Snowdonia, A Historical Anthology
– David Kirk. 60 writers portray the people and landscape of one of the most beautiful regions in Europe. 248 pp; ISBN 0-86381-270-8; **£5.95**

All the Days were Glorious
– Gwyn Neale. George Gissing in North Wales – quotes from Gissing's letters and diary. 56 pp; ISBN 0-86381-286-4; **£2.95**

The Land of Old Renown – George Borrow in Wales
– Dewi Roberts. A retrace of George Borrow's journey through Wales. ISBN 0-86381-436-0; **£4.50**

Both Sides of the Border
An Anthology of writing on the Welsh Border Region by Dewi Roberts. ISBN 0-86381-461-1; **£4.75**

A Tour in Wales by Thomas Pennant
An old classic abridged by David Kirk. 176 pp; ISBN 0-86381-473-5; **£5.75**

Revd John Parker's Tour of Wales and its Churches (1798-1860)
Abridged by Edgar W. Parry. ISBN 0-86381-481-6; **£4.75**

Places & Poetry

The Laugharne Poems
– Thomas Crowe. Poems by the first writer since Dylan Thomas to work from the boat house. ISBN 0-86381-432-8; **£4.50**

Skywalls – A Snowdonia Sequence
Poems and paintings by Clyde Holmes. ISBN 0-86381-466-2; **£5.75**

Walks with History

If you want to experience the very best of Wales, then these are the books for you. The walks are graded and there is something for everybody – short walks for families and more demanding routes to satisfy even the most experienced hillwalker.
Whether you choose to walk the high grounds, explore the beautiful valleys, study the varied wildlife or visit the remains of ancient castles and forts, the points of interest will explain what makes each area unique and help you choose the right walk for you.

Walks on the Llŷn Peninsula
PART 1 - SOUTH & WEST – N. Burras & J. Stiff.
ISBN 0-86381-343-7; **£4.50**
This series combines walks with history, stories and legends. Pastoral walks as well as coastal & mountain panoramas.

Walks on the Llŷn Peninsula
PART 2 - NORTH & EAST – N. Burras & J. Stiff.
ISBN 0-86381-365-8: **£4.50**

Walks in the Snowdonia Mountains
– Don Hinson. 45 walks, mostly circular, 96 pages, inc. accurate maps and drawings. 96pp ISBN 0-86381-385-2; New Edition: **£3.75**

Walks in North Snowdonia
– Don Hinson. 100km of paths to help those wishing to explore the area further. 96pp ISBN 0-86381-386-0; New Edition; **£3.75**

New Walks in Snowdonia
– Don Hinson. 43 circular walks together with many variations. This book introduces you to lesser known paths and places which guide book writers seem to have neglected. Maps with every walk. Pen & ink drawings. 96pp ISBN 0-86381-390-9; New Edition; **£3.75**

Circular Walks in North Pembrokeshire
– Paul Williams, 14 walks, 112 pages. ISBN 0-86381-420-4; **£4.50**

Circular Walks in South Pembrokeshire
– Paul Williams, 14 walks, 120 pages. ISBN 0-86381-421-2; **£4.50**

From Mountain Tops to Valley Floors
Salter & Worral. ISBN 0-86381-430-1; **£4.50**
Detailed information for casual/family walks and for the more adventurous walker.

NEW FOR 1998:
Circular Walks in the Brecon Beacons National Park;
ISBN 0-86381-476-X; **£4.50**
Circular Walks on Anglesey; ISBN 0-86381-478-6; **£4.50**
Circular Walks in Gower; ISBN 0-86381-479-4; **£4.50**
Circular Walks in Central Wales; ISBN 0-86381-480-8; **£4.50**
Circular Walks in Gwent; ISBN 0-86381-477-8; **£4.50**

Regions of Wales

'THE STORY OF . . .' Series
Wendy Hughes interweaves history, tales and events with attractive and interesting locations that will captivate and excite the visitor, leaving the reader breathless and surprised as she turns back the tide of time and glimpses into each century.

The Story of Gower. 88 pp; ISBN 0-86381-217-1; **£3.75**
The Story of Pembrokeshire. 100 pp; ISBN 0-86381-253-8; **£3.75**
The Story of Brecknock. 104 pp; ISBN 0-86381-316-X; **£4.25**

Radnorshire – A Historical Guide
– Donald Gregory. Radnorshire in many respects is Wales in a microcosm – hilly, wild, beautiful and small with the past ever present.
168 pp; 0-86381-284-8; **£4.50**

THE MICHAEL SENIOR SERIES – *A widely published historian with a series of well written volumes about different areas of North Wales.*

The Conwy Valley – Its Long History. 48 pp; ISBN 0-86381-035-7; **£1.50**
Llandudno's Story. 32 pp; ISBN 0-86381-391-7; **£1.75**
Anglesey – The Island's History. 64 pp; ISBN 0-86381-389-5; **£2.75**
Conwy – The Town's Story. 32 pp; ISBN 0-86381-345-3; **£1.95**
Caernarfon – The Town's Story. 32 pp; ISBN 0-86381-346-1; **£1.95**
Llŷn – The Peninsula's Story. 48 pp; full of illustrations; ISBN 0-86381-443-3; **£1.95**
Meirionnydd's Story. 64 pp; full of illustrations; ISBN 0-86381-442-5; **£1.95**

The Crossing of the Conwy
– Michael Senior. From prehistoric times to the new tunnel.
112 pp; ISBN 0-86381-191-4; **£3.75**

North Wales in the Making
– Michael Senior. A guide to the area's early history. Hard-back.
128 pp; ISBN 0-86381-322-4; **£9.75**

Two Bridges over Menai
– Robin Richards. History of the construction of the bridges across the Menai Straits. ISBN 0-86381-387-9; **£2.75**

This Valley was ours
– Eileen M. Webb. History of Nant Gwrtheyrn as remembered by one of the village's children. ISBN 0-86381- 428-X; **£7.50**

Place-names

Place-names of Dee and Alun
– Hywel Wyn Owen. 64 pp; ISBN 0-86381-325-9; **£3.75**

Place-names in the 3000ft Mountains of Wales
– Terry Datt. 180 pp; ISBN 0-86381-282-1; **£4.50**

A Guide to Welsh Place-names
– Anthony Lias. Over 500 examples giving meaning and analysing in a simple and concise way. 110 pp; ISBN 0-86381-289-9; **£3.50**

Cynon Valley Place-names
– Deric John. ISBN 0-86381-472-7; **£4.50**

Pronouncing Welsh Place-names
– Tony Leaver. Featuring Instant Guide to well-known names.
ISBN 0-86381-482-4; **£4.50**